DIVORCED KIDS

DIVORCED KIDS

Children of Divorce Speak Out
and Give Advice to:

- Mothers
- Fathers
- Lovers
- Stepparents
- Brothers and Sisters
- Boyfriends and Girlfriends
- Each Other

by Warner Troyer

Harcourt Brace Jovanovich, New York and London

Printed in the United States of America

LIBRARY OF CONGRESS CATALOGING IN PUBLICATION DATA
Troyer, Warner, 1932–
Divorced kids.
1. Children of divorced parents—United
States—Interviews. 2. Broken homes. I. Title.
HQ777.5.T76   1980   306.8′9   79-3531
ISBN 0-15-125748-5

Set in VIP Caledonia
First American edition 1980

B C D E

For Peggy, Marc, Scott, Jill, Jennifer, John, Peter
and Anne Troyer

Acknowledgments
To all the divorced kids. This is their book. And to
Glenys Moss, whose research, perception and
support made it possible.

Contents

DIVORCED KIDS

Introduction

This book is about the children of divorced families—and it is very largely *by* those children. The substance of what follows was distilled from hundreds of hours of tape-recorded conversations; the bulk of these interviews were with children of five to fifteen years of age but some, as indicated in the text, were with adults—former children-of-divorce now in their twenties, their thirties, forties, even their fifties. For these last, time has lent perspective, if not objectivity.

What ends between these covers began as a personal search: I have, from two marriages, eight children. At the time of this writing the youngest of those children is five; the eldest is twenty-eight. When this undertaking began I did not know how they felt about the two separations which had, respectively, disrupted their lives. As I began to think about that and to survey the literature I realized such children had been *written about* but not *listened to*. More than a decade after Dr. Elizabeth Kubler-Ross made the world aware of the great need of those among us who are dying to communicate their feelings there was still, I found, another silent fellowship in our midst—an enormous group of individuals unable to share, communicate, understand, exorcise their anxieties and their resentments. So I set out to record those views and experiences, to develop a kids'-eye-view of divorce and its consequences for the most-concerned but least represented parties to that act.

In practice my mission has been a bit like that of a travelling bartender for youngsters; someone they are unlikely ever to see again, someone who does not know, and will never meet, their parents, friends; someone to whom they can spill out whatever they feel, confident the disclosures and the indiscretions are safely buried in a tower of Babel built from other confidences and confessions.

The hundreds of children interviewed were astonishingly candid, delightfully articulate, starkly moving; they also, I felt, revealed a great and unnoticed failure of our society. You may make your own judgment on that as you read what follows, ranging as it does from the hilarious to the tragic.

A word about method and structure. All of the children interviewed, including my own, are anonymous; excepting my own, each was interviewed privately and without the presence of either parent; no parent has seen any transcript or excerpt of any conversation with their own child. Although I have tried accurately to describe the individuals and their immediate ambience, I have changed and disguised names, neighbourhoods, parental names and occupations, even cities. Given the way in which various interviews have been parsed and divided between chapters, and the time-lapse between tape-recording and publication, it's possible many of the children would now not be able to isolate or identify their comments.

But for divorced parents who suspect they hear the voices/ experiences of their own children in what follows, the answer is: they may, indeed.

First, in interviewing young people sixteen years of age and up I frequently taped interviews without first discussing this project with a parent, or securing parental permission.

Second, generally only one parent was involved in arranging any interviews although I was aware, on occasion, of the custodial parent discussing the matter with the absent spouse before agreeing to a taping appointment.

But third, and most important, the experiences and perceptions of the divorced kids in this book are sociological short-hand for the experiences of such children generally. If they ring true it will be because they reflect the universal reactions of these kids, at least within my fairly broad sampling.

As I mentioned earlier, the interviews have been thoroughly "scrambled," insofar as that was possible without doing violence to the reactions of the children. Sometimes, where it was a responsible exercise, the experiences of two children with similar perceptions are lumped under one Christian name; occasionally one child's views are split, presented under two different pseudonyms. So no parent should, reading this book, accuse their child of indiscretion or disloyalty; it would be hurtful, unfair, and probably wrong.

On the other hand there are a handful of horror stories in the book where, because of the explicit nature of the anecdotes, it's likely the parents may identify themselves despite changed names and places. Good. In these instances they deserve to. I apologize to the children involved if they feel embarrassment and hope they will forgive me; they will understand that their experiences could not have been masked further without entirely distorting the meaning of the events.

A final apology, if it is needed. This had to be an intensely personal document; the children's candour demanded a like response. I hope no one has been hurt thereby.

PART ONE
The Divorce

"Mommies and Daddies should stay together. They always should. They shouldn't never break up. Not never. I don't know why, but I know. They shouldn't. And I don't want to have kids when I'm big. 'Cause. Not never."

Candy is five. She is not keen on being asked to explain how she came by her views, but they are clear, forthright, fixed. The above passage came at me in a cohesive chunk—unedited and unequivocal.

But Mommies and Daddies do break up. It's a hard (and harsh) fact, in Western industrial society, that more than one marriage in three will fail. As world populations cluster in urban masses the figures for our huge cities—New York, London, Montreal and Moscow, Berlin and Toronto—approach one marriage in two. In California, there are now as many divorces as marriages. All in all, a huge and growing chunk of our population springs from broken homes.

Single-parent families comprise far and away the greatest problem for social workers and family courts in Western Europe, the United Kingdom, the U.S. and Canada. Moreover the problems engendered by divorce are acute and unique. Even the early studies now becoming available are too numerous to cite here and are, anyway, outside the mandate of this book. But it's worth reporting a couple of specific findings:

In New York City, where (as in all of industrial society) more suicides occur during adolescence than at any other time in life, *two of every three teen-age suicides are from broken homes*. And in England, studies released in 1978 said *children of divorce have shorter life expectancy, higher mortality rates, more illness, an earlier school-leaving-age* than youngsters from intact families.

Two conclusions seem obvious:

1. Marriage is now among the most fragile of our social institutions.

People who take enormous pride in their ethical or moral codes speak matter-of-factly (even proudly) about "serial monogamy." Marital contracts, far from being indissoluble, are now more often regarded as transient instruments. One of our greater social riddles revolves, now, around the question of how to begin conversation with an acquaintance not seen for a year or more: one must never open with "How's your husband/wife?"

because there may well not be one any more. So gaucherie-beyond-repair is avoided with a formula more appropriate to our life and times: "Well. What's been happening with you since we last talked?"

The extraordinary fact is that people with "happy" marriages of some considerable duration often feel obliged to explain why they're not divorced. "We were lucky," they'll confess. It just wouldn't do, after all, to be thought the sort of spouse who has been living an unexamined life, who has missed noticing that people are bound to grow in different directions, come to need and deserve new stimulation, new perception, new partners.

2. The consequences of marital breakdown for children are substantial, often traumatic and largely unstudied or passed over.

That's not to say or assume that marriages kept "intact" are necessarily best for children; often these "products" of unhappy unions need freedom from the agonies of unhappy marriage even more than their parents. They (the children) frequently see divorce as an end to pain rather than a prelude to fresh hurts. Society, however, still pays lip-service to a notion that divorce is aberrant. So *all participants in divorce, including the children,* pay a social price for their condition.

The kids, of course, often see our changing norms differently. Witness this description, by a five-year-old, speaking in portentous tones to a three-year-old, of the facts of life:

"What happens is, a man and a lady get to meet. And they get to fall in love. And they get to marry. And they buy a house. And they get to have some kids. And they get to be divorced. And they live happily ever after."

And then there's the four-year-old I met who greets each child he meets with: "Hi. My name's George. Who do you live with? Your Mommy or your Daddy?"

George was too young to be cynical; he was merely refreshing. Society, though, for good or ill, clings to the family as the basic unit of moral and social probity: and because we lack the sophistication to cope with dual moralities (inside and outside of marriage) we impose bone-cracking pressures on our divorced kids. Nor do those pressures begin with the decree absolute; they start in the first hour of separation.

1
Break-up

Recollections of "how it happened" range from memories of relief to those of profound shock—with shock well ahead of every other emotion.

At seven-and-a-half, Lawrence is a grave child who speaks very slowly, gazing intently from large, brown eyes, through blond bangs. He has been living alone with his mother and older sister for a year.

"I think they just choosed that. Daddy just moved away. I think he just didn't like something about them living together, so he just moved. I'm just kind of angry at him; I think he told her there was something he didn't like about her for a long time, 'cept he didn't cry when he left; my Mom did all the crying. We tried to get our minds off it by doing stuff we liked; but sometimes I can't get my mind off it and I think about it when I shouldn't, like in school. I'm kind of angry that he doesn't live here any more."

Ruth is twenty-eight; her mother and father separated when she was eight:

"I woke up late one night, maybe about midnight. I heard a noise downstairs and I crept onto the stair landing; Daddy was taking suitcases outside and then he came and took out a dresser. Mommy was in bed. He didn't say anything and neither did I, but I think he saw me. Mommy didn't tell me he wasn't coming back until a long time later—maybe a couple of months."

Alice was fifteen when we talked, four years after her parents separated:

"They were having another one of their arguments one night, after supper. Then, before I realized, Dad had just left. I thought he had just gone for a drive, but he didn't come home. The next day Mom sent his clothes and stuff somewhere in a taxi.

"I was so pale; then I started to cry and I just couldn't stop. The sobs just kept coming. It was a kind of emotional breakdown. No matter how much comforting I got it couldn't warm me—I was so cold."

Glynnis is fifteen; she was nine when her parents separated.

"One night Dad wasn't there; but that wasn't unusual; he used to travel a lot in his work. Anyway, the next morning Mom was up early, and she packed all his clothes, in cardboard boxes, and put them in the front hall. Then she went in the kitchen and packed another box; she let me help. She put in one cup, one glass, one knife and fork and spoon and one plate—and an old pot and a frying pan. She said all that stuff was for Dad but she didn't say why.

"Then, at noon—it was in the summer holidays—Dad came home and Mom met him in the front hall and told him to put the boxes in the car; then she told him to tell us what he was doing. He was pretty upset; he said he and Mom had decided not to live together any more and he'd see us soon. Then he said he had to go back to work, and he left. Mom went to her room and cried. We all cried, too. But we really didn't understand what was happening."

Of course, it's not always Dad who leaves. Jean at nineteen, has been living alone with her father for two years:

"I was staying over at my girl-friend's house. When I came home, the next day the other (three) kids were all staying at friends' houses too. The house seemed empty. The pictures were off the walls, the dining-room furniture was gone; my room—it had two sets of bunk beds in it—had only one bed left, just one dresser and just my shoes and clothes hanging in the closet. It was like a haunted house. It was really strange, I'd never had a room alone before."

Helen, now fourteen, was twelve when her parents marked New Year's by splitting:

"New Year's Day they had friends over with their two kids. Then my dad went off with the woman friend and didn't come back until five o'clock. He was drunk. The woman's husband was passed out on the chesterfield . . . and there was a big argument and everybody was hollering at everybody. And then Dad walked over and he just pulled down the Christmas tree and all the balls broke and everything.

"I didn't cry once, through the whole thing, except once, later, when we were having dinner that night and my Dad called my Mom a bitch. I took my chicken and threw it down on the table and ran upstairs. I don't talk about it now, I don't think about it, because I'm happy now. I sort of forgave my father. I don't remember anything now, I don't remember the arguments. The only thing I remember is New Year's and the time I threw my chicken down. And I sort of forgave my father. That time he called my mother a bitch, he came upstairs and said, 'Don't hate me'— and he was crying. And the next morning, my Mom packed and we moved away."

Jack, Helen's older brother:

"I didn't know what to think, really. I was just stunned, just stunned. I didn't really think it could ever happen. I didn't see it coming. It was just—bang." (He snaps his fingers.) "Just like that. She was gone and had her own place . . . When I came in that night, the Christmas tree was knocked over, not picked up or anything. No one really told me what had happened, what was happening. So I just went along. Then somebody told me they'd had a fight . . . I couldn't do much about it."

Sometimes, elaborate plans have been made and carried out before the children are aware that a separation is coming.

Hugh was thirteen when his mother decided to leave his father. He and his brother are now in their early twenties:

"I just came home from school one afternoon and there was a taxi waiting at the house and the driver was putting some bags in the trunk. My brother was already in the car. We lived in Mexico then, near Mexico City. And my mother said for me to go to the toilet and come and get in the cab, that we were going on a trip. And about an hour later we were on the plane and the next thing I knew we were at my grandmother's house, in Chicago. And then my mother told us we weren't going back. And that was it. I've never seen my father since, or heard from him. I don't even know if he knew we were leaving and Mom's never said a word about it. But she must have planned it for a while—she had the plane tickets all made-up, in her purse, and all the arrangements made."

When Victor was ten his mother evicted his father, *in absentia*; he's thirteen now:

"Mom packed some bags for my Dad one day. He was going away on a business trip. Then, right after he went to the airport, a man came and took the locks off all the outside doors at the house; and he put in new locks and chain things on the inside of the doors. Then Mom told my brother and me that Dad wasn't going to be coming back.

"And that night, after we were in bed—I guess she thought we were asleep—she phoned him, in Vancouver. And she told him not to come home. She said he couldn't get in and she'd call the police if he did. And she said her lawyer would fix him. And he didn't come home. He did what she said."

All children have some period of shock, surprise, at the separation; but some are more ready than others; occasionally, it seems, more ready than their parents.

June was almost twenty when she spoke; it had been just over three years since the exorcism of her father:

"It was a long-drawn-out affair. He was drinking a lot, had a real problem with alcohol. He'd come home drunk on the weekend and she'd say, 'Out!' And he'd go, and come back the next day, or the day after.

"Sometimes he'd hit her; slap her.

"Anyway, they were at a wedding—we all were—and he came back riproaring drunk. And then my mother came home and he went to punch her. And I stepped in the middle, in between them, to stop it. Then there was a taxi waiting for money and I had to run around trying to get the money. And I'd just had it: there I was, I mean, scrambling around trying to find money for the taxi, and them screaming—I was really ticked-off.

"I just couldn't be up all night, refereeing fights between them and go to school the next day and pretend nothing had happened. You couldn't even tell yourself nothing was happening. I'd got to the point where I'd just had it. And like, *we* couldn't go—so he just had to go. Like, I knew which side my bread was buttered on; like, there was no way they could live together, no way to solve the problem. I think my mother would have exhausted those avenues and there was no way to get my father into some kind of counselling; he wouldn't go, not even for the drinking.

"So, after that we had a big family council, sort of. The whole family" (Julie has one older brother, four younger siblings) "was there—a lot of yelling and screaming and everybody getting it out of their system. They all said how they felt about it; that we would all be better off if he left, if he just wasn't there.

"I think he was hurt. Like, he'd suspected it 'cause I'd been having a lot of hassles with him—we all had. But, like, I think he didn't want to accept it, didn't want to believe it. But he had to, when we all told him. And he left—that night. Never came back. Never has. They aren't divorced, don't need to be. I don't think he would ever try to come back. I think my mother has made it perfectly clear how she feels. We all did. That night."

Violence is the exception in most of these separations, though less exceptional than might be expected among well-mannered folk. The perception of it varies with age and with after-the-fact descriptions given youngsters by their parents. Anne and Charlene are four and six years old; both are blonde, like their mother; chubby, like their mother; garrulous, like their mother. They insisted on being interviewed together:

Charlene: "I dunno why Daddy moved. I think maybe because Mom decided she didn't want to live with him any more."

Anne: "No. It was 'cause he bited her. Daddy bited Mommy."

Charlene: "Well. Mommy bites us. She gives us love bites a lot, after our bath."

Anne: "But Daddy really bited Mommy. He hurted her."

Glenda is nine years old, her manner sober, reflective, her speech hesitant, with the underlay of a nascent stammer. Her face is very thin, pale, almost pinched-looking, her arms and legs and body very thin and white. Her bronze-coloured hair falls softly to her shoulders and curls a little at the ends. She wears boy's denims, a pale blue, sleeveless jersey, blue sneakers and socks. She listens with great concentration, seems very serious about answering fully and accurately.

"I don't really remember my father; Mom told me we've been living together (alone) since I was about three.

"She told me he sometimes went out, like, drinking, and then he came home. And then he was, like, shouting, and throwing things, and breaking things on my mother.

"And then he got really mean to her, and she moved away, with me.

"I never see him. I haven't seen him since we were divorced. He never phones me or anything. We don't know where he is and he doesn't know where we are, 'cause we moved."

Ellen is five; she is very blonde, very assertive, very round-faced and pretty, with large, brown eyes:

"The last time I saw my Daddy was on my baton day. And I never went to baton lessons that day. My Daddy went away and he said he'd be back at seven-thirty and then my Mommy came instead and she and my grandmother tooked me away to her place. And I didn't see my Daddy any more; and I didn't go to baton lessons any more and now I can't see him.

"But that's 'cause he disturbed everything. He went—he threw my hamster away and he threw my clothes away and he threw every one of my toys away. He did that last month; when I was tooked away to live with my Mommy and my grandmother.

"And I lived there; I lived with him. But then, when he tooked me there, I couldn't see my Mommy. He wouldn't let me. But now I can't see him, too.

"He threw everything away because my Mommy tooked me away, and I loved him very much. I even loved Mrs. Wiggins; Mrs. Wiggins is my hamster, he threw away. He was mean.

"They don't love each other, my Mommy and Daddy. They

married; and then they didn't like each other and then they just wanted to live apart. They were finished with all that.

"And then my Daddy tooked me away. And then he threw out Mrs. Wiggins. And then my Mommy tooked me back again."

Loss or destruction of pets is a recurring theme in these conversations; frequently it causes the sharpest and most bitter feelings among divorced kids. One variant on the "Mom/Dad got rid of our/my dog/cat/hamster" theme was told me by a twenty-three-year-old who heard the details from his father several years after the divorce, having lived through the first instalments with his sisters and brothers:

"We had two dogs and three cats. I was twelve. There were seven of us (kids) altogether. They split very suddenly and it was quite a shock. For all of us.

"About a week after Dad moved out, Mom sent one of the dogs in to the vet to be spayed. And as soon as that one came back she sent the other one; and while the second dog was still at the vet, being castrated, she sent in all the cats—all three of them—and had them done, too.

"And while all the pets were being sterilized, you know, Dad came to the house to pack the rest of his stuff. And while he was in the den, packing files and papers, we were sort of visiting with him, just talking. And he'd say, 'Where's Charlie?' Or, 'Where's Buster?' and we'd tell him they were at the vet, being 'fixed.'

"What I found out later, from him (and Mom told me the same story a long time later; she thought it was funny, too, then) was that, for several years, Dad had talked about having a vasectomy, and Mom had refused. And then that day, when he had heard about all the pets being sterilized, she went into the den and told him she'd been thinking, and maybe he should have a vasectomy after all. And he laughed at her and then he said, 'Where? At the vet?' "

Willie is fair, freckled, open and unreserved:

"I don't think they ever fought, I mean physically. But they really hollered a lot; and if Dad had a few drinks he'd do something violent—but not hit anybody. Like, once he picked up this really heavy coffee table while she was shouting at him; and he just threw it against the living-room wall, about fifteen feet away. With one hand. And it split.

"He was really hard to wake up; I think they fought about that the most. She'd holler at him to get up and he'd holler back that he *was* up, and swear and stuff. And then he'd go back to sleep; and then he'd blame her 'cause he was late.

"So one morning, she was really giving him hell. And he was in bed. She re-set the alarm clock, I guess, and when it went off, the second time, he just picked it up and fired it at the wall across the room. And it went right through and fell down inside. And he said, 'If you can't be decent, to hell with you.' And he left. Right then. He came back later to get his stuff; the next day.

"I brought my friend home from school the next day and we sneaked into the bedroom and put our ears against the wall, down by the floor, and we heard the clock; still ticking. Later Mom just patched the wall, covered it with wallpaper. Then we sold the house and moved here. I guess that clock is still down there in the bedroom wall."

These various stories of the split wouldn't be complete without Harley's, which, not to disappoint, fits the "B" movie, pulp magazine pattern down to the last tawdry particular. It was not the only such tale I was told.

Harley was sixteen at the time of the events he described, eighteen months ago:

"I was visiting a friend one afternoon, after school, and Mom phoned and told me not to come home and spoke to my friend's Mom and asked could I spend the night there and just go straight to school the next day. So I did.

"Then, at noon the next day, she came to the school and found me in the cafeteria, and took me out to her car and told me what was happening. It was all very cool. She was very calm, not crying or anything like that. She just seemed kind of mad.

"She said she found a grocery list in Dad's shirt, when she was doing the laundry, but it had all stuff on it that we hardly ever had—shrimp and fancy stuff. And she said she was suspicious, so she searched his dresser, and she found some keys, like house keys or apartment keys, she'd never seen. So then she took the keys to the hardware store and they made copies for her. And then she put them back and didn't say anything, but she gave them to a detective to use to follow Dad.

"So then, the night I was told to stay away, she went with the detective and a lawyer and a photographer, and they used the keys to get in and took a picture of Dad in bed with this woman, in her apartment; but I guess he was paying for the apartment.

"And then, the next morning, when I was at school, she put all Dad's stuff in green garbage bags and sent everything to his office, in a taxi; a whole taxi full of stuff in green garbage bags—and he had to pay for the taxi when it got there.

"It was a complete surprise to me; I'm not sure why she told me so much about it; it was really a shock but I was kind of impressed with them both. I mean, with him, partly, 'cause he was doing all that and we had no idea—just thought he was working late sometimes or something. He was always just the same at home, until she threw him out.

"And she kind of impressed me too, she was so calm. And she sure was tough, the way she investigated him and everything. Sometimes I kind of wish I didn't know quite so much about what she did—I mean the pictures and everything; she even offered to show them to me but I don't want to see them. I'm glad I know why they split up all right, but it's a bit awkward when I see Dad, knowing she's got those pictures at home, in her desk."

It's clear to me, in hindsight, that the greatest need for *all* children, when marital separation is inevitable, is for a period of adjustment. Even more than their parents, who have been living, in fantasy or reality, with the notion of separation for some time, these kids need some advance warning, some space in which to grasp the culture shock. I failed all of my children utterly in this regard. Normally I'm little given to any desire for chances to "do it all again, but differently," but in this area I'd give a good deal for retroactive opportunity to build cushions for my children against the stunning perception, after the barely-witnessed event, that I simply was not there any more.

My experience is not exceptional. Almost every child among the 300 to 400 with whom I talked complained they had been given no warning, paid no need in the all-absorbing terminal agony of their parents' marriage:

"I came home from camp and found out Daddy had been gone for three weeks. Neither of them even wrote to tell me."

"They sent me to stay with my girlfriend for a weekend so they could do it behind my back while I was away."

"It's like they were really ashamed and tried to pretend it hadn't even happened."

"My Mom lied to me. She said Dad was just away on business and, I was little, just ten, and I believed her. She just kept telling me that and she made him say the same thing for a long time. Then I noticed his stuff all seemed to be gone. I don't think I can forgive her."

"It's so much harder when it's a shock."

Shock is the common denominator. Only among a very few of the kids of divorce was separation expected; its pain was met by this handful with the relief felt after the extraction of a sore tooth. These children had two things in common: (i) regular experience of bitter and open acrimony between father and mother. ("Well, they were fighting all the time. I mean, I never heard them say anything nice to each other for years") and (ii) a peer relationship with a divorced child, usually a fairly sophisticated or dominant friend ("Harry used to come over to visit. And he'd say, 'Wow, look at your old man and old lady. They sure won't last much longer.' And I sort of got used to the whole idea even before it happened. Like, Harry was right.")

But for the overwhelming majority surprise left a numbness which soon triggered genuine anger at being "overlooked" by preoccupied parents:

"All Mom did for days was cry. Even for weeks, if I just asked what had happened, why they did it, she'd just burst into tears and run into her bedroom."

The general absence of any communication or discussion concerning custody adds to resentment. Here, though, the topic was rarely mentioned by youngsters under twelve; it was almost always volunteered by those over fourteen.

"It was as if we just went with the house. We were like part of the furniture."

"I don't know why we couldn't have gone, all of us, to talk to some professional, some advisor, to see which of them really wanted us, and what we wanted."

"With my mother, I'm sure it was a social thing. She thought her friends would think less of her if I lived with Father. She even gets upset if I say I had a good time with him."

"I felt like a piece of baggage and they just decided where was the best place to store me."

"Nobody cares what kids need."

Children are full participants in divorce. If our society grasped that single, visceral fact much of the pain evidenced here could be precluded for future kids of divorce; all of it would be eased. The youngsters know they are much more than observers, but they are kept in the role of stunned witnesses at a tragic traffic accident about which both friends were forewarned.

In twenty-five years of journalism I've encountered only one adult reponse that compares directly with that of these youngsters. It came from the recent widow of a man who'd died following a heart attack, after ten years or more of having kept his heart condition secret from her:

"That son-of-a-bitch," she ground out through a spate of tears. "He knew for years. Why in hell couldn't he have told me? Maybe I could have helped. At least I might have been better prepared. I'll never forgive the bastard."

Her rage was only the lining of her grief. But the parallel works unhappily well. Children need, deserve, have a right to be told what's happening.

2
Guilt

Gwen is about forty-five—intelligent, chic, well-tailored and well married—the contented mother of two teenagers, the chatelaine of a charming home. Her parents separated when she was five years old; her twin brothers were put into a foster home, she was raised by a grandmother. On hearing that I was writing this book she told me a little of her own background, then asked some questions:

"Are most of the kids you interviewed about the same? What was their most common reaction? Were most of them bitter? I don't think I was ever bitter, maybe because I was so young when it happened.

"I'll bet a lot of them expressed some feelings of guilt, though. I'll bet that was common. I always felt some of it, all right. I had some vague memories of my parents fighting over us, before they separated; I can't remember what about—probably expenses, I suppose, and money; that was during the depression, in the Thirties. And I think that was why I was sent to my grandmother's, and why they ended up in a foster home—because neither of my parents could afford to keep us. But I felt, all through my childhood, that it must have been my fault, because they used to quarrel about us.

"And then, about twelve years ago, I got a phone call one night, at home, right out of the blue. And the voice said, 'This is your mother, and I'd like to see you if I could, and get to know you.' And I'd never heard from her. I just couldn't handle it. There I was, with two kids of my own, over thirty years old, and I just couldn't deal with that call. I'd never seen her—I wouldn't have known her if she'd sat down beside me in a bar or a restaurant. I had this awful feeling, as if I'd been kicked in the stomach; I felt flushed and guilty and upset. And I thought, 'Why do I feel guilty? She left me.' But I couldn't help it. So I asked my husband to talk to her, I just couldn't bear to have that whole can of worms re-opened, after all these years.

"So he told her for me—it must have been kind of hard for him, too. And she accepted it and that was that. A few years later, she died, and we went to her funeral. I saw the twins, there; for the first time. I didn't feel any remorse, about not seeing her; but I still feel a bit funny about the divorce, and whether them having my twin brothers and me had much to do with it. I guess you never entirely recover from that sort of a shock."

A good deal of the estrangement between divorced kids and their parents stems from feelings of guilt and embarrassment in the children, which lead these youngsters to feel major constraints in spending time with parents whom they feel may blame them for the marital crash. There are, it seems, very few kids from seven or eight years and up who feel no responsibility whatsoever, even if the sense of guilt is largely unformed. This surprised me. It will certainly surprise anyone who expects the innocent to feel innocent. And the degree of guilt involved may surprise everybody.

Often, as with Andrew, the conviction of guilt is highly particularized. His story is not uncommon, indeed it's far more common than I'd supposed; parents seem more careless than one might easily believe about letting children learn facts which can hurt them in later life:

"They got married when they were really young, you know. And I don't think either of them really wanted to get married very much. They just weren't ready, and maybe they didn't love each other all that much, either. And they felt too young.

"But, see, Mom was pregnant—with me. So they had to get married then, even though they weren't ready. And that was really my fault. 'Cause I was the kid they had to get married about. And I don't think they were ever too happy together, liked it really very much. They didn't argue too much in front of me when I was little; but by the time I was five or six they seemed to be fighting just about all the time and they didn't seem to care much if I was there or not; I mean they'd just go ahead.

"But what I heard—from what I've heard, they sure wouldn't have got married if she hadn't been pregnant—Mom hadn't been—with me. Of course it's been a long time now—they were divorced when I was seven; but they still fight a lot, when they see each other. And I wonder about it sometimes, still.

"Like, what would have happened if I wasn't here? Maybe they would have got along better. Or maybe they wouldn't have got married—they wouldn't have had to, and they might have both found somebody they liked better.

"Boy, I don't know. But I'm sure never gonna get anybody pregnant. I'm not gonna get married unless we want to."

The most highly developed and detailed of all guilt scenarios is bound around memories of parental fights over the children. Most often, one child has been the focus of quarrels—usually a child whose behaviour has irritated one parent more than the other. Nothing could be more finely calculated to leave that child with an oppressive sense of having been the trigger for war.

Susan is sixteen. She has a seventeen-year-old sister, Wilma, a twenty-year-old sister, Lois, and a brother, Bruce, who is eleven. Their parents separated last year. Susan is tall and lean with very fair, very curly hair, cropped short; her manner and movements are what used to be called "tomboyish." She has the wide shoulders and large bicep development of the serious swimmer. Her speaking style is flat, matter-of-fact, clipped:

"I think kids should talk to each other about it; we don't that much. And parents should try to be nice to the kids in the beginning; they should tell them what was wrong and why they separated. 'Cause we might think it's our fault. And I think both parents, together, should tell the kids. So they'll be able to believe it.

"I kind of had the feeling my father was just tired of it all. He was always very quiet—a quiet man. And Mom was the noisy one. She has always done a lot of hollering. It was always my Mom who would hit us, and discipline us. You could tell Dad didn't like it. When he saw us doing something, he'd talk to us quietly and he would tell us that this wasn't right, or that wasn't. But she would always yell. And you could tell that it really used to bother him. It was every day, and I think he just got sick of it. We never heard them fight, much, but sometimes he'd ask her not to yell. But she'd just keep on yelling.

"So, I don't know if we were partly to blame because they had different ideas about how to discipline us. But you wonder, when they don't tell you. I could never ask them, 'cause I don't want to upset them. But I'd like to know."

Susan's sister, Wilma, a slim, pretty brunette, suffered throughout our conversation from what my eldest son, Marc, used to call "chin wobbles." She was deeply hurt, confused, by events since the separation and several times let tears flow, silently, unheeded. Her brown hair was in a high pony tail; despite the tears she maintained level, unwavering contact from wide-set, blue eyes:

"Parents should tell their kids what happened. Otherwise you can't help wondering. You know, maybe the disputes over you between them might have made it happen. They should really be open about it. I don't think it could be anything that's going to hurt the kids more than they already are, that's for sure.

"My Mom's been pretty open with me, I guess. I would like my Dad to have taken the time out to be open with me, to just sit down with me, explain why it happened. One thing is that kids, when it happens to them, should just accept it, and not feel guilty—that's not good. They should talk about it. I mean, not all the time, but it's good to get it out in the open—I even think probably it's good to cry about it if you're upset. (Wilma licked a stray tear from the corner of her mouth, brushed another off her cheek with the back of a hand, absently.)

"My sister Lois doesn't talk about it, at all. She just won't. But she's the one who seems the most affected of all of us. Like she's been going with this guy for about three years—I think they were pretty serious—and she broke off with him about a month or two after Dad left. She didn't say much except that he was always wanting her to talk about it, to explain and get it out of her system and she didn't want to.

"She heard about it by mail, in a letter from Mom, about three weeks after it happened; she was away at college, near Boston. I guess that's a pretty hard way to find out. And, see, she was the oldest, she was the closest to Dad, and he didn't even call her or write to her to tell her what was happening, what had happened. And, she didn't exactly say so, but I think, 'cause she was the oldest and everything, that she kind of feels that, if she'd been here, if she hadn't been away at college, she might have been able to do something. She just seems to feel totally involved, totally responsible. And then she's broken up with her boy-friend. He has called here and she just won't talk to him; she just stays in her room most of the time and won't talk or anything, just cries a lot; and now she's talking as if she might quit college, too—not go back this fall; and that's crazy. But you can't tell her, 'cause she won't talk. She's just, well, belligerent about it."

Linda is fourteen: "Mom and Dad used to argue about Laurie a lot. I think that really bothered her, too. And Mom would get really upset and be crying and everything all the time and Laurie would be pretending it didn't bother her, but you could tell it did. Usually Dad would take Laurie's side and Mom would be against them, and Laurie started to say that, like, it was really her fault they had such fights. And then maybe Dad would be out drinking with his friends, on the weekends, and you wouldn't know what might happen when he came home."

Says Linda's older brother: "Sometimes I think it'd be easier if you had somebody to blame. But there really isn't anybody. It's no good taking sides. I know that Laurie sometimes tries to take the blame, but that just makes her feel rotten. It would be better if they would both have told us why it happened, so she wouldn't try to take the blame."

Elena is, at seventeen, slim, self-possessed, poised and contained. She speaks softly, deliberately, without strident self-consciousness or difficulty with the intimate topic. Emotional pain is only a dim cloud at the back of her brown eyes:
"I was eight when it happened. I think they both thought we were all fine, that everything was all right. But I used to cry every night for the longest time. I couldn't understand what had happened, or why. I wondered if it was my fault somehow; I think little

kids are like that—superstitious.

"You couldn't say anything to them, though. Not then. They had enough to worry about and they thought we were OK. And I think we were, really. I mean, it was hard. But it happens to lots of people. Doesn't it?"

Hal is a rather reflective ten.

"It was OK between them for a while, I think. But Mom really isn't a very good housekeeper; you know, not very good at cleaning and cleaning-up after kids and stuff like that. Dad's kind of fussy about that stuff, too. So what I think is that it was OK between them until the baby sister came along, my little sister, Wanda. And then they used to fight about her, a lot.

"My Dad would start talking to my Mom about Wanda and then they would always start a fight. It was so stupid. My Mom started this stupid argument once, just before he left; I'll never forget it: Dad changed a diaper on my sister, my little sister, and my Mom started an argument about how he did it. I mean she just hollered at him for about an hour. And then, I think it was just about then, he moved out."

Wanda, now seven: "My Dad says he looked after me real good and my Mom didn't. He says she wasn't any good, looking after me. But I live with her, now. But she thinks it was my fault Daddy moved away, I think."

Here Jean gives her reasons for staying with her father. She is petite; her features are small and well composed, her forehead and chin still slightly marked, at nineteen, by acne; her hands and feet are very small, her hips slim, her build slight. She curled up comfortably on a chesterfield while we talked, one foot beneath her, never changing her posture during the forty-five minutes we talked. Jean borrowed a cigarette as we began—then chain-smoked from the open pack throughout the interview, her only physical sign of strain. Her air of controlled tension and her manner of speaking were both very much like her mother although she claimed her personality mirrored her father. We spoke in the living-room of her mother's apartment, which she was visiting, and she showed considerable nervousness whenever her mother walked past the room; her voice would drop, and her eyes; she would puff intently on her cigarette. (The mother, her hair a "new" colour, had lost forty-five pounds in the eighteen months since the separation; a very tense woman, her face showed the strain of the weight loss and of the post-separation tension.)

Jean: "I stayed with my Dad because I wasn't getting along with my Mom at the time, and part of the blame was being put on me; my Dad and I had very similar personalities and my Mom was pretty mad at my Dad...My Mom was always asking me, for months before she left, why I always sided with my Dad...Up until last Christmas I couldn't look at my Mom. I couldn't speak to her; there were too many memories of bad words.

"Some of their arguments were about me; Mom would threaten to throw me out a couple of times and my Dad didn't like that. I felt as if I was always starting another thing between them...And I knew some of the arguments could have been avoided if I had just walked away and ignored it. But she was always calling me all sorts of names and I couldn't just stand there and take it.

"You wouldn't know me from a year ago. I couldn't eat. My stomach was always upset. I almost failed school. I had to quit my part-time job. I was just depressed all the time; none of my clothes fit me because I had lost so much weight. I never smiled, never had a good time wherever I went..I got so I wouldn't go out at all, just stayed in the house all the time. I was just a real bore.

"I stayed with my Dad because I just didn't think he and my brother could manage. Neither of them could even boil an egg. They would have been hopeless alone. So I stayed with him. To help."

Finally, Lee, eighteen:
"They were always fighting over me, that was for sure. My father always used to call me the black sheep of the family, I was the one who started smoking first—who'd come in late. He used to say I gave him a pain. It was always there, between them. I used to avoid him a lot.

"My Mom used to say, 'Yes, you can do this,' or, 'You can do that. But don't let your father know.' So there were two sets of rules in the house, for me: his and hers. But I could only use hers if he wasn't there to find out about it.

"I used to think, 'Well, you're the mother in this family. Why don't you just stand up to him and say, "Let her do this." ' But she never would, not in front of him. I guess she figures: What if he left? I mean, she couldn't know what to do, maybe she was kind of frightened about it in a way, because she didn't have a job or anything. But then he did leave, anyway. So even when I tried not to make trouble between them, it didn't help.

"Once, I remember, I wanted to go over to my girl-friend's to sleep. And my Mother said, 'Yes,' and my father said, 'No.' And then I went, anyway, and when I came back the next day, it was a Saturday, they were in the kitchen. And they had this terrible, big silence. And he was glaring at me, and she was too, a bit, as if to say, 'Look at what you've done, at the trouble you've caused.' So from then on I thought, 'Okay, fine. I'll do what they want.' I suppose I wanted them to stay together, to stop fighting. I didn't want to be the cause of them separating. But they split, anyway."

There's a lot of talk and study nowadays about the need for "private" spaces; it's an ongoing concern for city planners, social scientists, educators, architects. Only after beginning these interviews did I develop a full sense of the other side of that coin—the need for our children to have privacy from *us*.

I can remember, now, too many times when a child's behaviour, desires, formed the centerpiece for wrangling between me and their mother, with them present or within earshot. Parents, before and after separation, owe it to their youngsters to carry on those discussions well away from the dangers/temptations of being overheard.

And parents, before and after separation, need to make the point to children that consensus in respect of the children's needs is real; sometimes those "pronouncements" should be made together; often they can be announced separately, but in a way that reinforces belief that both parents feel the same degree of love, concern, support for the child.

Parents often find more time for individual conversation,

concentrated attention with and for their children after divorce. The kids are frequently well aware of this phenomenon, and gratified by it. But it only works with devotion to ongoing dialogue by the parents, both parents. For these youngsters, as for you and for me, communication—frequent, candid, open communication—is the means of exorcising every fear and anxiety.

Andrew, at fourteen: "If they are going to get separated or if they are already separated the first thing is they should see that their kids get to see both parents at least once a week; otherwise it's going to be really terrible.

"What the kids should do is talk to their parents, both their parents, as much as possible, until they are really sure they haven't got any more questions about why the parents separated. You've got to try to keep close to both parents as much as possible and keep sure, in your own mind, that it wasn't your fault, 'cause otherwise you're going to feel like dirt.

"And don't listen to one side; listen to both sides. Because one side can make the other side sound like dirt and then you'll just get hurt and get confused."

Alma: "If parents have to split, think they do, they should be very, very careful, and not make any rash decisions, because they're really going to regret it.

"And they should tell the kids why they split; or else the kid will only form his own reason, which might be the wrong one, like I did; and that opinion could affect his relationship with either parent; he could be more bitter to one than the other.

"See, I think that parents are really selfish as far as relationships with the children are concerned. For example they seem always to tend to compete; each one wants more influence with the kids than the other one. And I think the kids are much more aware of this competition than the parents. What they've got to try to do is share the child, not use the child like a rope in a tug-of-war. There's been enough war, already, during the separation.

"The other big thing is to treat the child same as before the split; not be buying the expensive presents or trying to bribe the child, to win the competition, or making everyone uncomfortable by always doing some big number instead of just being natural.

"I think it may be because the parents feel a bit guilty about the kids—all the presents and things; we don't really like them. But I'm not so sure: 'cause it seems, too, that the parents are so wrapped up in themselves that mostly they forget all about the child. But it is important to be natural. Big deals, big gifts—the kids only get confused, wonder what's going on."

Anna, at nineteen: "You parents should let the children in on your feelings more; don't always think that because we are being polite or seeming to be OK that we don't care, or that it isn't our concern. It's our business, too, you know; it's our life, too.

"The main thing, about kids, is they shouldn't become too involved with one side or the other. Don't get caught in the middle, that's the worst—and both sides, your mother and your father, will probably try to get you to take sides. I mean, they both think they are nice people, right? And they'll want you to think so, too. So if you agree, then they think you're on their side.

"That's why I almost went crazy. There was always this conflict; first one would tell me something, and then the other. And kids find out; as they get older, it changes. When you are small then everything is black and white. Small kids all tell you they know in their hearts who is right and who is wrong; they have to know who they can blame when life is kind of tough for them. But then, when you get older, you understand more; you'll probably understand that both were right and both were wrong. So the most important thing for kids is to try to be patient, and not too jumpy, if you can."

Lindy is ten: "I'd tell kids just to not be scared. Because there's nothing really to be scared about—but it seems that way, the first few days, like when you go to the hospital. Try not to get too scared, even at the beginning. You'll probably feel better later. So you should try to wait for that."

Sharon is eleven: "I can't say anything to help for parents. Nobody can help them, I don't think.

"But if kids get upset when their parents separate then they should just not think about it—try not to think about what's bothering you. Specially at night, when you are in bed alone and your Dad isn't ever coming home to sleep with you. Just maybe, think other things; that your Mom might get married again someday. I wouldn't like that, though, really."

Larry is fifteen, and, like a good many teen-aged divorced kids, he's angry about how it was handled:

"You guys, parents, just go ahead and do it and don't even tell us what's happening, so we can be a bit ready. When we find out, poof! It's over. So maybe we think you're being so mysterious about it, not telling us anything, 'cause it's our fault or something and you don't want to embarrass us.

"And then you just tell us where we're going to live—maybe go to a different house, an apartment, different city. We just go along. No questions asked.

"I'm not sure it's much good giving parents advice. I'm not sure they listen. I'm not even sure, really, they care. Or they would listen, would tell us what's going on. Wouldn't they?"

Until this project began, I had been, I'd more-or-less imagined, a reasonable parent. Not, I found, by the yardsticks used by these divorced kids. I'd failed miserably in respect of at least half the criteria thought essential by the kids—and so, clearly, had their parents.

Some children, those thrusting their reactions behind a wall and refusing to acknowledge any relationship between the marital breakdown and their own lives and fortunes, denied they wanted consultation. One feared their iron self-denial of involvement in their parents' divorce would lead directly to much more intimate consultations with psychiatric professionals on their own behalf in later life. These kids, maybe one in twenty, were totally encapsulated and self-controlled and gave off almost visible vibrations of contained rage denied expression: "It's got nothing to do with me at all." "I don't care why they did it. It's their business." "It just doesn't matter. I don't care whether they get back together or not."

But with all the other children, of all ages and both sexes, there was anger or hurt that they had been given no sufficient explanation.

It's been an escalating source of chagrin for me to realize that I so thoroughly mis-handled this aspect of my relationship with the older children of my first marriage. It's hard to accept the monumental stupidity and pomposity with which I told those kids, the first few months after the marriage dissolved, "This is between your mother and me. I'm never going to give you any information about it, or criticize her, or answer any questions about this. That would be unfair to everybody. You'll just have to accept the fact that we've decided not to live together any more."

I even had the towering effrontery to brag to friends that I was "being careful" to avoid hurting the children by keeping them "out of the line of fire;" and when my wife and I found ourselves able to talk quietly about "how to deal with the kids," we would agree they should be kept in ignorance, "for their own good."

Our blindness was astonishing; and cruel, not any the less because it was uninformed. A twelve-year-old, Wayne, put it as well as any of the children: "No matter what, it would be better if they'd tell me why it happened. I mean, nothing could be any worse than what you imagine, if you don't really know."

And that's the nub; if the locus of this guilt syndrome can be defined, then, as with most other guilt, fear, superstition, anxiety, it must lie in ignorance. In all my conversations with children of eight or older, there were only two in which youngsters actually said they did not want more information on the causes of their parents' discord. Except where the causes were wildly explicit, every single child spontaneously expressed a deep need to "know why it happened."

The irony here, of course, is that often the parents don't know. Marital relationships are probably the most complex and difficult devised by our society; the roots of dislocations are rarely any less tangled than the web of associations within the marriage. Even where there is a proximate cause of break-down—infidelity, drinking, violence—it is most often merely a behavioural symptom masking a more fundamental problem.

So how can parents deal with the profound "need to know" expressed by these kids: well, most fundamentally, by negatives. Children should be told, and emphatically, that *they were not the cause* of the divorce. Children are often the most realistic members of our society. Control of their environment is exceptional to them—but they are prepared to accept and understand those forces over which they've little or no control.

So. Tell them. Children needn't be given transcripts from two years of marital counselling, analytic data on Dad's menopausal obsession with younger women, on Mom's frustration over his preoccupation with career and professional fulfilment. But *some* explanation. Some words to lubricate the transition. Maybe as simple as:

"We've changed. We both feel we would like to try living apart. We both love you as we always have; that won't change. But sometimes adults fall out of love. They don't regret what happened earlier, but they see the chance to do some things differently in the future."

Sound lame? Well, maybe. But it beats hell out of letting young people believe their parents regret all of their marital past, including their children. Beats, too, giving children to understand they have no right to feel angry, shocked, frightened by what's happening around them, and *to them*. Why shouldn't they? They've invested their whole lives, not just a few adult years, in that family unit. It's *theirs*. So they damn well should feel disappointed and, yes, angry.

Once more, *children are not witnesses to divorce; they are participants*.

That line should be engraved on the consciousness of every divorcing parent, nailed to the wall of every divorce lawyer, judge, social counsellor. Children don't just want to talk about what's happening, they feel a right to be told, to be consulted on where they will live, and with whom, to express their feelings about custody and parental visits.

It's an easy prescription to recommend, but a tough one for separating parents to follow, especially if the parents have no lucid notion of the "reasons" for their marital crash. Surely, though, the children deserve at least enough warning to fasten their emotional seat belts?

A bit more would help: it should be feasible for each parent, individually, to tell the children that their worth is unchallenged, their confidence in parental love accurate. There is, even in the most "civilized" marriage ruptures, a considerable air of anxiety, truculence, scepticism; more usually there's overt anger, rage, bitterness. Kids need to know none of that is directed at *them*. So friends and relatives need to rally around. (They often do so, for one or both of the parents. Parents, though, are likely to be sustained, at least in the short term, by the exigencies of their changing lifestyles and the ardour of their anger; it's the kids who, in the first days, lack even the support of righteous indignation.) But finally only mother and father can supply credible comfort.

In the last few decades I expect enough people to populate a small city have devoted themselves to the problem of explaining "the facts of life" to children. I only wish a dozen reflective folk had worked as hard at divorce education. More guilt is probably generated, in our society, by divorce than by masturbation, copulation or parturition. It's not that we need learned dogma. All it would take is a fraction of the attention given to forethought that we've lavished on foreplay; we just need to let the young people in our personal worlds know they are treasured and loved, let them know they are more than pawns and nuisances on the marital chessboard.

The best time to "level" with youngsters, this is all to say, is immediately. The best language to use is any that is simple, direct and honest. Kids know about pain; kids understand tears. They won't think you weak and undependable if you weep, show pain. Watch any five-year-old comforting a three-year-old with a scraped knee. We are here to hold another, and children perceive that more easily than most of us. But never to hold one another at arm's length, unless we wish deliberately to court and generate misunderstanding, fear and guilt.

Tell them. Any way you can. But don't freeze them out. They deserve better and need more.

PART TWO
Adapting

"Children are so adaptable; they have really adjusted beauti-fully."—from comments made by most of the parents of children interviewed for this book.

They certainly are. Adaptable. That's the rub. In the circumstances of marital break-up children are the fastest learners imaginable. Several months or years on, the shocks we've been chronicling have been lived through and assimilated, to a greater or lesser extent. But, like the once-burned cat, the children are now forever twice-shy. Trust fades. Their quickly absorbed lesson is the rule of "expect too little." Less disappointment lies in that direction.

Their gut reaction may range from bitterness to resignation, from rage to apathy or patronizing patience. But, for better or for worse, there is a thread linking the perceptions-of-future among all but the most favoured of such children: clouds are generally lined with cold rain; wishes are rarely granted; tooth fairies almost never find the right street address; and Dad will likely fail, again next week, to get tickets to the ball game or fresh sheets for the fold-away bed.

The most personally depressing words I've heard from one of my own children, after two failed marriages, were those of my six-year-old son, Peter. I had let him down in what, in adult terms, was a minor matter; I'd simply failed to waken and organize my day early enough, one "visiting" Saturday, to accommodate the activity which I'd promised the previous evening. We'd "have to do some-thing else, instead, because there won't be enough time for that now." Peter responded with more self-control, more grace and more gravity than should be possible in any child of six:

"That's OK, Dad," he said. "It doesn't matter."

But it did. Or worse, it didn't—but should have done. That evening I began recalling a whole series of those softly spoken absolutions from my youngest son. They filled me with remorse and, more vitally, with alarm. I didn't want my child to expect too little of life.

In the time between her third and fourth birthdays my young-est daughter, Anne, avoided the traps of apathy or resignation. When, after an extended radio taping, a crush of traffic and a failure to budget my time adequately, I arrived, an hour late, to collect her with Peter for the weekend, she was loving but direct, and indignant:

"Where were you, Dad? Why were you late today?"

Peter, leaning against a banister beside his younger sister while he pulled on his snow boots, interrupted the beginning of my explanation. His words tumbled over one another, rushing to stem the explanation that might only lead to renewed belief and hope:

"It's OK, Dad. Anne, it's OK. It doesn't matter. You don't have to explain, Dad. It's all right. We understand, don't we, Anne? It's all right. We had lots to do, didn't we, Anne?"

It was three days before I learned from the *au pair* girl that both children had waited outside, on a raw day, for forty minutes before returning to their TV program and their waiting-for-Daddy-who-is-late-again.

The lack of confidence in future gratification shows, especially among younger children, in more subtle ways. Asked what they'd "like to do today?" they may hesitate to name a preference; it's the carefully planned "treats," after all, that seem most precious and therefore vulnerable. Or they may opt for the same agenda as last week, the week before. More even than other young children, these intimates of disappointment will suggest a return to the same movie, a visit to the same park, a chance to re-climb the same hill; maybe remembered pleasures will be easier, safer.

Iola is eight years old. She has short, brown braids, hazel eyes, steel braces on her teeth; she is very shy, speaks with head averted. Her sentences tilt up toward the ends, avoiding any chance of being fastened to affirmative responsibility. While we talk she winds one braid, the right one, around her index finger; but it is too short to go round more than once. Time and again, just as she starts the second circlet of hair around a dimpled knuckle, the hair, used up, springs from her hand; she starts again, fails again:

"Dad travels all the time. For his job. He always writes to me and sends me postcards . . . Usually he does. He says he sends them more than I get them, sometimes. He says that's because of the post office. I don't know.

"But I like it when I get them . . . The last one was nice. It was Chicago. In the summer." (The interview was taped in November.)

Henry is fifteen. He is slim, compact, well-muscled and co-ordinated. His use of language is good, his mind quick, but he will hesitate twice, even three times before finishing a short sentence so that coherent thoughts sound choppy and unformed. His bed-room is tidy, well-organized, the walls covered with posters, calendars, plastic models, photos of his parents, brothers, sisters. His voice, probably newly-changed, seems too large for his frame or his age. Perhaps he is aware of the incongruity and this may explain or contribute to his halting way of talking. Often, in the pauses, he laughs; the laugh is forced, almost a bark or cough, the self-conscious laugh that is half apology, half designed to distract from more pressing inadequacies:

"It's best not to—plan too much—about the future or what you are going to be doing.

"Like, Dad always wants—to go on a camping trip—every summer—with me. We did—once; before they were separated, I mean. But he really works hard—to support everybody—and everything—so up until now we haven't actually gone—camping. Something has always come up—every summer; well, it's only been three summers—since the divorce.

"So, anyhow, it's not fair—is it? To depend on them too much. Not fair to them—if you understand—to make them—feel there is pressure about this stuff—because they may not think—that you understand when they can't make it."

In the following three chapters we'll look at three key areas in which almost all divorced kids have to adapt: community perception that they have "lost" a parent; holidays and birthdays; economic constraints. We'll see how they feel about the changes and see how they cope.

3
Losing a Parent

One of the toughest areas for divorced kids is their self-conscious awareness that everyone knows they are minus one parent. Despite the ubiquity of divorce, we still haven't lost a sense of stricture; the attitude that "two parents is normal" runs deep. And divorced kids, as we shall see, hate more than anything to feel set apart, noticed, pitied because of their parents' separation.

For the very young, though, it can be less of a problem. Sometimes adaptation can seem almost spontaneous. As with most four-year-olds, Jennifer is not interested in being "interviewed." But she is as articulate as she is spunky in her blonde pony-tail, Snoopy sweater, blue jeans and red sneakers:

"My Daddy doesn't live here now...But we don't need no Daddy; my Mom cuts my meat. I can do it, too.

"A man takes the snow (from the driveway). He gots a truck. Daddy didn't gots no truck. He gots a car, though. We don't. Not now.

"When Daddy comes I sit in the front. He gots a nice car. We don't.

"Daddy doesn't love Mommy now. I go to see him, though. Sometimes."

Few teenagers find it so simple. Tony was fourteen when we talked; his parents had separated four years earlier. He is dark, slightly built, of average height, intense—his hair almost to his shoulders, his eyes rarely making contact during conversation, his big-knuckled hands constantly in controlled motion, massaging one another, stretching and cracking one knuckle after another. We talked in his bedroom. The furniture in that room of about two metres by three comprised a narrow single bed pulled roughly "straight," a small, battered dresser, a table lamp resting on the floor, sans shade. Some games and models were stacked on dresser top or floor mixed with a number of long playing records and a scattering of discarded clothing. The wallpaper was Victorian and faded.

We sat on the bed to talk, side by side, not looking much at one another. One sneakered foot pressed and twisted against the floor monotonously, as if to grind out a cigarette or crush an insect. Tony's manner and mood throughout our lengthy talk were that of someone unused to self-expression, uncomfortable with the subject, but ardent to express his gut feelings at least this one time and, best of all worlds, to a stranger from whom he need accept no judgments nor fear any retribution. Tony has two (younger) sisters. He is not doing very well at school; his mother declares herself unable to cope or communicate with him. "I just can't understand what's wrong with him," she complained. "He just doesn't seem to care about anything." Tony puts it differently:

"At the start we were s'posed to see him (Tony's father) every week; it was like that sometimes...We see him every week; well, we used to—some of the time. He's pretty busy. It doesn't matter ...

"I just get so mad at them (his sisters) sometimes; or at Mom. I don't know why. It's not important. It's just that the only time we talk it seems like is when something's wrong or somebody's mad...

"He sees us pretty often. But he's pretty busy, I guess because he has to pay for his own apartment and everything now and send Mom money, I guess... and he's got this girl-friend; I mean, she's usually there...

"And then we, all three of us, usually visit him at the same time. So we don't talk much...We never stay over, hardly. But that's OK. There isn't room at his place...

"You have to decide things yourself. I mean nobody can do it for you, or help you or anything. But everybody's like that, I guess...

"But sometimes I feel mad at him. I mean, why am I supposed to miss all that stuff? I'm scared. I don't know what I might do...

"But I guess it'll work out. I don't know."

Cynthia is ten: "I feel sad 'cause I can't see my father any more. I'm not sure what he's like. I'd like to know him. I haven't seen him since I was five.

"Maybe he tries to send me presents, like on my birthday or Christmas presents, but he just doesn't know where I live. I think he'd like to, if he could.

"But I don't like it. At school, they have this day, for fathers; and you have to bring your fathers and see whose Dad is best. I couldn't go. I haven't got a Dad. And sometimes they ask your mother and father to come to school so they can talk to them. And my mother can't go, she has to work; and I haven't got a Dad.

"On Father's Day—well, I've got a Grandad—and I've got—I've got a man, a man that I really, really know; and he told me to call him 'Poppa.' I met him at the school, in the yard. I've got a lot of uncles, too. And sometimes I make them a Father's Day card, and my Grandad, and the man who said I can call him Poppa. I give them the cards we make at Father's Day; my teachers don't know I don't have a Dad. That man that I call Poppa—he's really a nice man. His wife died.

"When kids ask if I have a father and I say, 'No,' they tease me. That makes me feel bad. So I mostly don't tell them. I'll just say, 'Yes.' Or else I'll call my Grandad over; and I'll say, 'Here's my father.' He doesn't mind. Or sometimes I'll play that the man I call Poppa is my Dad. He doesn't mind either. I don't know his real name. It's better that way. You don't like to spread it around; that you haven't got a Dad."

Wendy is nine: "I make my Dad a card at school for Father's Day every year. And I bring it home. I've got three cards, now, in my room. I'm keeping them. So if I ever see my Dad again I can give them to him."

Caroline grew up in Christchurch, New Zealand; she is twenty.

Her parents separated when she was twelve and, an only child, she stayed with her mother and moved, three years later, back to her mother's family home, in England:

"I certainly had some sense of guilt. I think, mainly, it was because of the society where we lived. You see, New Zealand is a pretty old-fashioned place, even though they may think they are progressive. It's what you'd call a Victorian society, or maybe an Edwardian society.

"So when my Dad left, I really felt embarrassed, felt guilty, as though I had some ugly skin rash or something, that all the other children could see and be disgusted about. Divorce was regarded as a social disease in New Zealand. And it didn't matter that it was your parents who were responsible for the disease, you were blamed, too.

"So when we came back here, to England, and I had a new school and new friends and everything, I pretended that it had never happened. And when I filled out the first form, at my new school, and it had a space for, 'Father's name,' I just wrote in, 'Deceased.' And everyone was very nice about it, and I didn't have to feel guilty any more. I said he was killed in Viet Nam, because I had a girl-friend in Christchurch whose father was wounded there."

For Georgina, at eighteen a nine-year veteran of divorce, the embarrassment still lingers:

"When you go over to your friends, when the fathers are there—well, the fathers always treat you so well; I mean, they treat me too well. I feel funny. I can remember last year, we moved, and I went to the new library to get a library card, I was seventeen. And they asked me what my father's business was, when they were filling in the card. And I said, 'Well, I don't live with him.' And you could just sort of, well, feel all the eyes on you. Maybe I'm just over-sensitive."

Lisa is twenty, short, dark, stocky, feisty: she's smoothly co-ordinated, darkly tanned, short-haired:

"What makes me maddest is that people seem to think they should just sit around, after three years, for God's sake, telling me how sorry they feel for me. Why can't they just be natural and good company? If there's one thing I don't want it's to be looked down on or felt sorry for. That is the thing that's always bothered me the most; I could never stand that. I would rather you hated my guts than pitied me."

Linda is eleven; she's been a divorced child for two years:
"Some of the kids at school come up to me and say, 'Tut, tut.' (She smacks her lips in a superior sort of way.) 'You should see how nice it is to have a father living with you,' they say. But I guess it doesn't really bother me. I just say to them that it's not my fault they're separated; and they did used to live together."

Andrew is twelve: "Sometimes someone could make a joke about it. It's happened to me before—mostly at school...And then I kind of get jealous of the other kids—who've got Dads."

Doris is nine; she is too serious for her age, with no laugh lines, dark of eye, of hair, of spirit:
"At school, maybe some kid might go and tell everybody about it and maybe after school, like at 3.15, they might—everybody might make fun—everybody'll make fun of you and everybody'll say, 'Oh. You don't have a father, you party pooper.' And then they'll start swearing at you and calling you names. They'll say, 'You baby, 'cause you don't have a father,' and all that kind of stuff."

Eileen is twenty-eight; blonde, slim, attractive, successful in her career in publishing. She hasn't married. Eileen grew up in Rhodesia, she and her sister spending much of their early life at boarding school. It was during a holiday, when she was eleven, that her father left.

"He left, really, very late one night; just packed his bags and moved out. But that evening, before he went, he told my grandmother why he was going—or why he said he was going. And I was there, in the room with them, so I heard it all, too, as he knew I would. Mommy was out somewhere that night; he was gone before she got home but I guess she must have known what he was going to do.

"What he said was that he had found out that Josie, my younger sister—she was nine then, and she was still away at school that week—he said he'd found out that he wasn't Josie's father, that my mother had taken a lover, years before, and that he was Josie's father—the lover.

"Of course that was ridiculous. Mommy was a church mouse right until she died. But he was sure of it and he said he never wanted to see my Mommy, or Josie, ever again.

"All her life, Josie could never understand why Daddy never wrote to her or sent her birthday or Christmas gifts. I could never tell her why and I never will. Even if Daddy had been right it had nothing to do with Josie. But she has suffered for it, all these years.

"Now he's getting pretty old and the woman he's been living with all these years would like Josie and me to write him more often and visit him; his heart is bad. But I feel uncomfortable with him. When Mommy was dying he knew and never wrote or came to see her. And the only time I guess he's ever seen Josie was at the funeral—when he finally came, too late. And even then he didn't say a word to her, not even acknowledge that she was there; it was a crazy scene; I couldn't believe it.

"I will never be able to understand how he could have behaved so badly. He's really quite a decent and kind man. Or so I had always supposed."

Running through the vast majority of the conversations is the faint, diffidently-expressed hope for reconciliation. Most children are careful to qualify the wish, maybe fearful of bursting their fragile bubble of hope:

Wilfred, at fifteen, after six years' separation:

"When I was younger I wanted to see if they could get together again. I thought I could—I wanted to try to get them together. But right now I know that I can't. They, uh, they just don't get along. Some people do. Some people don't. But I just can't—I don't know how to do it. I used to dream about it, that I might find some way to get them together. Then everything would be OK. Really OK. Not any more though. I don't dream about that now. Not very often."

Elmer is six; his parents separated a year ago; he and his eight-year-old sister live with their mother. They see their father, for an afternoon, every second Saturday.

"I don't like it. I used to like it better when my father came home every day. Now I don't like it at all."

Candy is a very poised, rather thoughtful five-year-old: red-haired, hazel-eyed, snub-nosed—pert and engaging:

"Well. It's different. I have my own room now. But I miss my Daddy. Very much, too. I can't do nothing about that, I guess. But I wished I could. Get him back."

Tandy is sixteen, has had an absentee father for two years:

"I don't think it's changed me at all. The separation, I mean. Not deeply, I mean. Not really.

"Only my two closest friends know about it. Nobody else. Well, I guess my teacher knows about it. My mother went and told her after I had a bit of trouble with my school work. Sometimes I don't exactly pay attention to my schoolwork and I just get day-dreaming. (About a year after the separation, Tandy was twice in trouble with the police because of neighbourhood vandalism; she and some friends threw some paint on a house front; another time they ripped up a neighbour's flower bed. In one year, Tandy went from a straight 'A' student to a near failure at school).

"I s'pose sometimes I daydream about them getting together again; I don't think I can do anything about that, though. But sometimes it makes me mad a little bit—makes me frustrated. I feel as if I could just break something, and then, suddenly, every-thing would be all right; or I'd feel better, at least.

"My Mom said she'd like to get married again, sometime. But I don't want her to. I guess that's not fair. But my father is my only father. My real father. I don't think I could accept anybody else. I'm pretty OK about it now, though. Not affected much."

Lesley is eight; she was six when her parents moved apart and has not seen her father since. She has an air of waiting, of stillness, watchfulness. Her hands were in constant motion as we spoke, twisting a small, flowered handkerchief out of all recognizable form.

"My Dad might come, someday. Or he might have died, I don't know. When I'm older I can look for him; I can look in the newspapers and I can ask people, like pen pals, if they have seen him; they could write and tell me.

"If I saw him I'd be really excited. I wouldn't be mad with him, I'd just be sorry 'cause maybe he tried to see me but he thought maybe I was dead, too. Or he didn't know where I was to send me anything.

"And I know what would happen. We'd meet, and he'd hug me. And I'd hug him. And he would say, 'I'm sorry. I wouldn't do it again. Do you and your mother want to be together again?' And then he'd say, 'Ask her tonight when you go home and I'll be waiting. I'll wait somewhere.'

"And I'd ask her. And she would want to be together again. And he'd be waiting. And I'd go and get him. And he'd come home.

"I think he might say that. Do you think so?"

Lastly, Fay. Fay's parents have been divorced for three-and-a-half years. She has never heard from her father, or seen him, since the separation. He lives about thirty city blocks from the apartment she shares with her younger sister and her mother. Fay is ten years old; she has dark hair, hanging straight to her shoulders, grave, brown eyes, a slim, athletic build, an almost perfect cupid's bow mouth with a small, attractive mole on the left side of her upper lip. She is quite breathtakingly lovely in her childhood, and serious far beyond her years.

"The first Christmas, after my Dad left, I wondered why he didn't come and see me, or send me a present or something. And on my birthday. Later. Mom said she guessed he'd moved away. Or he was pretty busy.

"Then, last year, she said she thought he had probably died, maybe somewhere in the States. (Helen lives in Montreal.) So I'm not surprised any more that he doesn't care about my birthdays. I'm really sorry he's dead. He was nice.

"When I grow up I'm going to save my money and work. Then I'll write to people, in the States, and try to find out where he's buried. Then I'll go and put flowers on his grave.

"He was nice to me. I wish he wasn't dead. Sometimes, at night, I cry when I think about him. In bed. I really miss him. But I don't talk to Mom about it. She must be sad, too. Even though they divorced. It's sad, though."

Fay's mother had spoken, by telephone, with Fay's father (about alimony payments) the day before I recorded that conversation. Her mother thought it was "better for Helen" to believe her father dead, since he made no efforts to see her. I wonder.

Children make their own adjustments, as do we all. But if we can't help them, we might at least get out of their way, stop building extra hurdles with our overwrought perceptions of divorce, our silly "sympathy" for their "condition."

We could even help. We could talk to young people about the changes in our society; we could share our confusion and concern with them, let them know we don't feel in possession of all the answers, either; we could tell them there is no inherent evil in divorce; that guilt-by-association is utter nonsense, that confused people, hurt people, are not bad people.

The loyalty of children to their parents, both of their parents, in almost every conceivable circumstance, is a miracle that makes man's footsteps on the moon seem commonplace; if you doubt that, talk with any official in your community who has interviewed children, especially small children, beaten or battered by one or both parents. The wondrous thing about a child's love for a parent is the acceptance. More than any valet, our children know our weaknesses, our failures, our fragility. But when they love us, they love us for our reality and seem to sense that, if we can cope with our lack of perfectability, they, too, can hope for fulfilment despite their vulnerability.

Divorced kids will accept a less-than-perfect world; they must. They'll do so more philosophically, though, with more hope and joy, if we let them know they've not been diminished in our eyes by the confusion in society about divorce. They wear their stigmata, these divorced kids, inside their eyelids. We can help them know the brands are spurious, cosmetic, phoney, and we can stop "protecting" them from guilts that never should have been.

4
Special Days

About one child in every three with whom I spoke spontaneously mentioned that holidays were the toughest times for them. When asked, all of the other children agreed. For many divorced kids, one in six at the least, "special" days bring double trauma: first the strangeness and pain of a recurring special event which has now lost much of its joy; but beyond that, these particular kids find themselves mourning one anniversary while trying to celebrate another—because a very large number of marriage break-ups occur during or immediately following festive times, when emotional strain is greatest. The staff of any hospital emergency ward or psychiatric facility will confirm that by far the greatest number of suicide attempts take place around Christmas, New Year's, Valentine's Day, birthdays or wedding anniversaries. In shaky marriages, as with shaky personalities, the pressures of emotionally significant days can shatter all restraints on the dark impulses to self-destruct. It's probably true that more marriages crack at the Christmas dinner table than in the marital bed, though the fracture lines may extend deeply into other areas of family life. So for divorced kids holidays are rarely a time of unmixed joy.

It is also through holiday periods, with the shuttle celebrations common to many divorced children, that they begin to develop areas of sophistication far beyond their years. It was this characteristic, noted at Toronto's International Airport, that first led me to consider writing this book.

I had been in Europe, filming, for several weeks in late

November and December. Returning home via Munich, Zurich and New York, I'd marvelled at the lovely German toys and picked up some small gifts for my children in a Munich shop, just six days before Christmas. So, on the flight home, my thoughts were much on the children of my first marriage, who would be arriving for their annual yule visit on Boxing Day, and the two children of my second marriage which was to rupture just after Christmas, a year later. I was travel-weary when I boarded the Toronto flight at Kennedy Airport in New York and, wanting to rest, chose the very back seat on the aircraft.

About twenty minutes after take-off a carefully dressed, rather pale young girl of nine or ten paused by my seat while waiting to use the rear toilet.

"Do you like the back seats?" she asked me. Tossing her long brown hair a little with a jerk of her head, she indicated the forward part of the cabin. "There are a couple of empty seats up there, just over the wing. That's where it's the smoothest. It's usually much rougher back here in the tail, you know. And it's always much noisier."

I thanked her for her interest, then her turn at the toilet arrived, and she was gone. A bit later, looking for a magazine in the forward book rack, I noticed her again, in earnest conversation with an elderly gentleman who was her seat companion. As I passed, he was saying, "Yes, I'm going home to visit my son for Christmas."

Two or three rows ahead was a boy of about her age; like her, he was turned out in his Sunday best, a blue blazer, grey flannels, a white shirt with a tartan, clip-on bow-tie hanging loose at one side of his open collar. He was engrossed in the vista from his window, had an empty seat beside him strewn with comic books, and seemed, like the girl, to be travelling alone.

On arrival at Malton's terminal I stayed some time in my seat and was the last passenger to disembark. Just a few steps ahead were the two children, both in the care of a stewardess who was evidently taking them to the baggage/reception area, where each was being met.

There are two terminals at Malton, just north of Toronto. The newest, imaginatively called "Terminal Two," can be an ordeal for a tired passenger carrying heavy hand luggage; it is about 400 metres from the loading finger at either end of the building to the ticket and baggage facilities. As luck (and Air Canada) dictated, and as pessimism had taught me to expect, our plane had coupled with an exit ramp at the second-last finger of the northwest wing.

As we walked rather slowly down the interminable, broad passage, the little girl turned to the boy walking beside her and remarked,

"I don't know about you, but I really prefer to fly American Airlines rather than Air Canada when I come to visit my Mommy, because American flies into Terminal One. It's so much more convenient; because it's round, you see, and you don't have to walk nearly so far; and you can just take an elevator to the car park. Besides, American flies from LaGuardia in New York, and it's a lot closer to Manhattan than Kennedy, where you have to go on Air Canada. But I really don't like Terminal Two, here."

Our lives parted again as we separated. But that little girl's face and voice stayed with me all through that Christmas holiday. I can still see and hear her; still marvel at her worldliness, at an age when skipping ropes and scooters seemed more appropriate than DC-9s and luggage carousels. That was the point at which I began to wonder whether, like fraudulent antique dealers, we beat our children with emotional chains, scorch them with social blow-torches, to add the scars and patina of age and use.

Christmas has become so widely observed as a commercial and social holiday in western industrial society that it is generally marked by children from families of all faiths, or no faith. New Year's has less significance to most children, who aren't yet peering at the downward slope of their years. So for them Christmas and birthdays are the events most anticipated, most enjoyed, most remembered; second only to these come the annual school holidays with possibilities of a camp, a cottage or camping trip, or of days at a city park, beach, swimming pool. It's from the texture of these occasions that divorced kids most easily recall the festering slivers of disappointment and disillusion. In childhood, disasters are often unrecognized by anyone else; agony can dance on very small, easily missed nerve-ends.

Ellie, fourteen: "Dad left last Christmas Eve. It was really crazy. In the morning he was here, and then he didn't come home to wrap presents that night; he didn't come home at all. On Christmas Day, when we were all worried about him, he telephoned, from Mexico City, to wish us all Merry Christmas; and to tell us he had left Mom that day. He was down there with his secretary. And we were supposed to have a Merry Christmas. I hung up on him, before I started to cry."

Jacquie, fifteen: "On Christmas morning, while we were opening our presents, my Mom phoned, from Los Angeles, to wish us Merry Christmas, I suppose. My Dad hung up before we could talk to her and we couldn't call back because we didn't know where she was staying. He said she shouldn't interfere with our Christmas, that we'd be seeing her next week anyway, when we visited her."

Lisa and Georgina recall, four years later, the first Christmas after the break-up; Georgina was fourteen then, Lisa sixteen.

Lisa: "It felt weird, really weird, the first Christmas he was gone. You see, we always had a Christmas ritual: my father used to sleep on the couch in the living-room, right beside the Christmas tree, to make sure we didn't get at the presents until after we'd all washed and had breakfast—all eight of us. My sister, Georgina, and I used to come down and see what the tree looked like, with all the presents, after we went to bed on Christmas Eve. And then we'd sneak back upstairs again. Of course the really neat thing was to tip-toe around the tree and have a really good look, without disturbing Dad, or wakening him up.

"Anyway, that first Christmas I woke up about four o'clock in the morning. I just couldn't sleep, I was so excited on Christmas morning. I sneaked in to see the tree, at four o'clock, without thinking; and I was thinking, 'Now, I mustn't wake Dad up'—and then I saw the empty couch, beside the tree, and I remembered that he wasn't there any more. I went back to my room and I put my head under the covers, and I cried for a while.

"I think we all really felt it that Christmas, except maybe Mom. I think she was pleased. But it was hard for everybody else.

"My oldest sister was living on her own, in an apartment, and she cooked a Christmas dinner for Dad. So I went over there, we all did, all the kids, after our Christmas here. I felt I had divided my time equally, then. But it was pretty hard with him, too. Pretty emotional. Because Christmas had always been a big deal for him—especially with so many kids."

Georgina: "Well, that first Christmas was really bad. It felt so strange here, without him to hand out the presents and make everybody wait their turn and all. The presents we had got for him were just left under the tree, after everything was opened, by themselves. I think quite a few of us maybe had a little cry, privately, in our rooms, after we opened the presents.

"So then, after dinner, we brought his presents over to our sister's place, to see him and give him the presents. And at the end, after he'd opened the presents from us all, he just started crying. It was pretty bad for a while. I felt really bad about it.

"But then, after we got off the bus, on the way home, I just told myself, 'That's the way it has to be. You can't change it or anything.' And I couldn't. So you learn to accept it. We still go over every Christmas, in the afternoon, after we've had our Christmas dinner with Mom. He doesn't cry now, so it's easier."

Mary, who is twelve, and her fourteen-year-old sister live with their mother. Their seventeen-year-old brother, Richard, and nineteen-year-old sister, Lillian, live with their father:

Mary: "We went to my Dad's for a few minutes on Christmas morning, and he gave us some presents. Then we said 'Merry Christmas,' and we went home. Next Mom took us to my Grandma's—her mother's place—and everybody on my Mom's side of the family was there, and we had Christmas dinner there. I didn't like it much."

Richard: "Christmas seemed pretty funny this year. I mean without the little kids running around, and playing with their new toys and stuff. They came over for a little while, in the morning, and got their stuff from Dad and us; it wasn't so much this year, because there isn't as much money. And then they just went home. A bit later Lillian and I went to see Mom, and took her a present. But it was queer, with us all going back and forth. We stayed for a while—about an hour or two, I think. And then Dad cooked a turkey for just the three of us, for Christmas dinner; but it was really quiet, kind of spooky, while we were eating it and everything."

Lillian: "Just after the split-up there was Easter, and then Mother's Day, and then my birthday and my two sisters' birthdays and my Dad's birthday, and then Christmas. It was just too much.

"And Christmas was so different. When we were all together we'd all get up, about seven o'clock in the morning, and by about nine o'clock all the presents would be opened and the turkey would be cooking, and we'd mostly have the day together, just our whole family.

"But this year, Richard and Dad and I didn't get up until almost noon. It was like we didn't want to wake up and have it be Christmas. We didn't have much money—we opened about three little presents each, it just took a minute. And my sisters came over for a few minutes. And then they left.

"And then my Dad just started taking the decorations down off the tree, after they left. And that was it—Christmas Day was over—except we ate, later. It was my Dad's idea to take the tree down. He didn't say anything—just looked at the tree and then started to take everything off it. And I started helping him, didn't say anything, either. In an hour it was done and the rugs were all vacuumed and the tree was outside, in the garbage can, and it was like a normal day, except we didn't work and we had turkey for dinner.

Lillian's birthday, a few months earlier, hadn't been an unqualified success, either:

"It was just after they split; I had to go to school that day, and when I came back—Dad didn't even come home that day—after school, I found this card that they'd left for me, I guess, but didn't want to see me, or talk to me. And what they'd done, they'd just stuffed some money in a birthday card and wrote, 'Love, Mom and Dad'—which was phoney. It just didn't seem like anything. I mean, money! I'd always had real birthday presents. It didn't matter if they were big or expensive, because we never had that kind of money in our family, even before the separation. But the thing was they had taken time and thought about getting something I really liked, that I suited, always before. And I'd always had

64

birthday parties and thousands of friends over, and hot dogs or spaghetti or sandwiches and cake and ice cream. And they always seemed to care, you know, and to find time to make it really special.

"And now, all of a sudden, it seemed like it was really an effort for them just to find a lousy card. I guess I was really hurt. I felt mad, but mostly I think I was hurt."

Winston, twelve: "Before my birthday every year, Mom says she'll come to Dad's house and take me for lunch, to the revolving restaurant downtown. It's her birthday, too, the same day. Before I came to live just with Dad she used to say I was her best birthday present. And now she says we should celebrate together. But it's been three years now, I think. And she can never make it, since she moved in with this other man and left my Dad. I get a present instead; it comes in a taxi."

Lawrence, seven: "My Mom said my Dad could come to my birthday party this year. She wanted him to take some pictures of the party for us to keep. But then they had a big fight at the party and some of the kids went home. It spoiled my birthday. Next year I hope my Dad doesn't come to my birthday."

A wistful footnote from nine-year-old Mary:
"I have a girl-friend who is divorced. But her Dad sees her Mom—not like us. When it's her birthday, she can have it at home with both her Dad and her Mom. That's really a nice way to do it."

School holidays, summer vacations, frequently involve games of human "hot potato" with the youngsters shuffled between relatives, camps, trips to absolve either parent from responsibility.

Mollie is four: "I like to have my holiday with my Dad best. 'Cause he gives us apple juice. And we can go out in his garden and get some sun-burn and he puts up an umbrella for us. And there's swings and slides near his house, when we have our holiday."

And Mollie's brother, Ivan, at five:
"We get two birthdays, and two Christmases. But Santa Claus only comes once; to our house, where Mommy lives."

Mollie: "We only got a little bit of stuff, though, at Daddy's house. But the holidays are good. Not so much Christmas. The apple juice is good."

Wendy, eighteen, a divorced kid since age seven:
"My Dad had this cottage close to the city, still has it. And he'd take me there for the day, in the summer. As I got older sometimes he'd keep me overnight.

"But there were always so many people at the cottage, his friends and his girl-friends and everything. And they'd all be talking and doing things together. I guess he figured that just because I could go for a swim or something I didn't have to be amused, I was just a kid. And he had to entertain his grown-up guests. So we never really got to talk much there, or visit or get to know each other. It was like, he had me there, didn't he? That was enough."

Ward, at sixteen: "It's been about ten years now since the divorce. The first few years my Dad used to take us on camping trips and, a few times, on canoe trips. Once I went alone with him and that was the best; I got to know him a bit better. But then he started bringing his second wife along; and I don't think she liked camping very much; she was always too cold, or too wet, or the ground was too hard to sleep on or the fire wouldn't cook properly. It wasn't much fun, with her along, and he and I never got to go fishing in the evening, or anything.

"Then, three years ago, he broke up with her, too. He was in a pretty bad mood there, for a year, and we didn't have a summer holiday with him. This year we did—but now he's living with this other woman; she's really nice, but he doesn't want to do stuff with us now—he just seems to want to be with her all the time, even when we're there."

Hal is ten. "I got pretty mad at him once, but I didn't tell him—at Easter, one year. We were out on a picnic, and it turned out my Dad had already arranged tickets and everything to take my sister and me to Florida. I said, 'Are you kidding? Does Mom know?' And he said she did. Then he went away somewhere for a little while, walking around and that. When he came back he said, 'I just phoned your Mom again and it's okay; you can come.'

"So then we drove back to the city, got on the plane and went to Florida for about seventeen days. Then we came back and when I went to the school, one of the teachers said, 'How come your Mom phoned to see if you were at school?' I said, 'I don't know.' I really did know, but I wasn't going to tell her about it; it wasn't any of her business.

"So then I knew about my Dad not telling my Mom about it. What he did, I found out, was he phoned her from Florida on the Tuesday; the picnic was on Sunday, when we flew to Florida. And my Mom had phoned the school on Monday 'cause she didn't know where we were. I always have been mad about that. Like, it was a lie. I don't lie to him."

Jack, seventeen: "The worst times are the special times: like at Christmas and in the holidays, in the summer. 'Cause people make plans, my Mom does, and they count on them. And then things happen, things go wrong. For instance, maybe a cheque doesn't come. And so you can't leave for your trip or something. You can't ask your Dad about the cheque 'cause he's having a holiday, with his girl-friend, and you don't know where they are. So you just have to not go.

"Sometimes, on important occasions, I'd say, 'Do you have the cheque?' and sometimes he'd say it was in the mail or sometimes he'd say he was waiting for his commissions, his pay. But it was like he was lying to me and I think he knew. I mean, I think he knew I knew."

Holidays, birthdays, religious festivals provide special opportunities to express love to children, to build their confidence in continuing emotional security and stability. There's no mystical formula needed at such times, just the same awarenesses of human need we've seen the children describe.

There are, from what they've told me, some obvious rules-of-thumb:

It's hard for children to believe they are much loved if their separated parents can't, on the occasion of the child's birthday for instance, set aside rancour long enough to share in some aspect of the celebration. ("I don't see what's so terrible about us all having lunch together on my birthday." "Daddy came to my party but he and Mommy had a fight and he didn't stay and see my cake.")

No one wants to be the object of a dispute; and divorced kids have finely-tuned nerve ends: they know, when each parent competes to deliver the most lavish Christmas, the most exotic holiday, that they've once again become counters in a complex web of one-upmanship.

For children, predictability spells security. Routine is most comforting of all. If a particular star always went atop the Christmas tree it shouldn't be thrown out just because "your Dad made that stupid thing. I've never liked it." There's no reason why traditional school holiday retreats should be avoided after divorce. The accompanying parent has to face up to social reality anyway—turning adult insecurity into a burden for one's children won't hasten the process.

I can recall many constrained telephone conversations with my children on their "special days"—conversations that certainly did more to heighten their discomfort than reinforce their joy. I think I realize, now, that it's OK to let one's children know they are specially loved and missed on festive days, to ask children what they'd most like to do, where they'd most like to be at those times. Most of all, I know now it's too easy, and cruel, to allow children to infer parental hurt because a child is with the other parent for a significant day. Silly, too.

It's ironic that children are so often hurt by parental desire to avoid communication with the other spouse. I learned, slowly, to stop being reluctant to call my kids on the 'phone for fear of enduring an argument with their mother or interrupting their time with her; learned, too, to quit making them feel guilty when, while staying with me they wished to call her during a special occasion—or at any other time. It's a lesson slowly absorbed but worth the effort. The reward is in their eyes, and their voices.

5
Money

For almost all divorced kids there has been a cut-back in lifestyle, a tightening of economic constraints and a reduction in options, be they about clothing, holidays or just "treats". Often the changes are masked, for a few weeks, a few months, a year or more, by a parent determined to over-achieve, to "make up for" the emotional trauma with material gifts. Witness Greg, at age seven, in the first year of his divorced state:

"My Mom is buying me a new two-wheeler; I've already got a two-wheeler bike, but she's going to buy me a ten-speed. And we'll give the old one away; I've had it for a year. And we got a new record player; and a new TV, a coloured one. My Mom buys me lots of neat stuff."

Greg neglects to add, or perhaps, to notice, that his "new apartment" is in a public housing project where his mother moved to take advantage of the subsidized rental system; it's a far cry from their former home, a four-bedroom, ranch-style bungalow set in a spacious, treed property.

Liz is twelve and reflects both aspects of the changes in lifestyle— the reduced housing standard on one side, and also the "splurge" syndrome which seems to characterize a need to "nest," to signal fresh beginnings and, perhaps, to "show him" (the former husband) that the family can cope very well without him, thank you.

"My Mom brought my Dad up here one, because they had to talk about us—about what we were going to do in the summer... And she brought him in the living-room and gave him some tea and showed him all the new furniture. And then they just sat there, and I just sat there. And he looked at all the new furniture and so did she. But nobody said anything about it. They just sat there and hardly talked at all.

"The new stuff is OK. But I'd really like to live in a better place. This apartment is OK; it's the best we can afford, now. But the house, our house, was bigger and older. Someone's bought our old house, though; and Mom's getting money from Dad for it. I guess that's good. We need the money."

A digression: probably more than half the interviews I conducted were with children who had experienced a separation within the previous three years; and in more than half those homes there was clearly a substantial amount of new living-room/dining-room furniture. What was curious was the consistency of style in the furniture: it was almost all heavy, very solid, massive—almost Gothic. Because coffee tables too large for the rooms where they are placed and looming, dark cabinets give off an air of permanence and security? If I were a furniture salesman I suspect I could spot a shopper as a recently divorced woman after about thirty seconds.

Andrea is eight, and has been separated from her father for almost two years. She lives with her mother and two other sisters. An older brother is attending college in Colorado.

"We had this neat house, with a big swimming pool and everything; and we all had our own room. But the bank took it. Dad had this business, they made stuff for computers, and he made Mom sign something, at the bank, before he left; he didn't pay. The bank fired everybody at his business, and they took the house too. And we moved. And Mom bought a smaller house, at first. And then we all helped to paint it, and she sold it. And then we moved to this apartment. It's not very nice. It's really hot and none of us have our own rooms any more. When Charles came home for a holiday he had to sleep in the living-room.

"Mom has a boy-friend now. He has four kids, too. And he has this big house. I hope she moves in with him and then we could all have more space."

Hank lives in a small, two-storey, brick home in a modest part of Vancouver. The main floor has a small entrance hall with stairs to the upper floor, a small kitchen, a combined living-room/dining-room about eleven feet by sixteen feet, and two small rooms at the back, behind the kitchen, each of which is about eight feet square. At a guess these back rooms were once used as a sunroom-cum-study or family room and a laundry room; now both are bedrooms. Hank shares one with Johnny; his nineteen-year-old sister sleeps in the other with her mother. Both rooms are very crowded, with two narrow beds each and a profusion of clothes on hangers, small tables, dressers, a chair.

"We have people living upstairs now. We can't use our rooms up there. So I sleep with Johnny. I have to sleep with Johnny now, and he makes a mess in the room. He won't be tidy. So I can never find any of my stuff. Because of the mess. And it's really noisy. The people upstairs make a lot of noise and it's hard for me to sleep. They have a really noisy record player. And one of them plays a guitar; with all that noisy loudspeaker stuff. So it's hard to sleep.

"Mom fixed it up upstairs herself. I helped her. And then we painted the walls here, too. She built us a new sandbox; and we got some tadpoles, in a big jar, to watch. But I sure miss my old room. It was upstairs, but I can't go up there now. Mom says we need the money. From the people upstairs."

We shouldn't imagine that paternal custody always solves money problems. Al is eleven and has lived with his father for two years:

"Whenever I want something, say a bike, Dad always says he has to pay the housekeeper so much money; and she wastes food, he thinks, and she uses too much soap and stuff. And he says she won't fix my clothes when they get holes or rips or something, so he has to buy too many new clothes. So it costs a lot more than when we lived with Mom, he says; and he can't make ends meet. So maybe I'll get my bike next year."

Children of divorce have a better-tuned ear for economic reality than most youngsters; and they cannot be distracted from their firm grasp of pragmatic fact. On one occasion, when I was trying to persuade one of my daughters that she could manage better in a mathematics course, she remarked quietly that "there hasn't been much extra money lately, and I don't have the textbooks I need, yet." (This following a period when I'd been late with support payments.) There was no trace of reproof in her manner, just a gentle (but devastating) reminder that it's as necessary for adults to face up to reality as it is for the children who are the "beneficiaries" of parental lapses and failures.

There is a profound difference, by age, in the perception by divorced kids of straitened economic circumstances. Very young children, those under seven or eight, seem largely unaware of such difficulties; generally they accept changes in lifestyle with total equanimity. Hamburger instead of steak suits them fine; and they seem much less aware of the quality of their clothes or their home. But between eight and about twelve there is an acute self-consciousness about financial status; clothing; spending money vis-à-vis friends and school mates. Witness Danny, at twelve:

"We don't have so much money now and I don't get an allowance, like I used to. So, after school, I always say I have to come home and do chores 'cause I haven't got any money to buy a drink or things like that with the other guys.

"And now, this year, I only have one pair of jeans right now. Last week, one morning, I tore them, so—Mom was at work—I had nothing to wear to school. So I stayed home, in the morning, and I patched them. Then I went to school in the afternoon, and I told teacher I was sick in the morning."

The financial strains seem less in larger families. Where there are several teenagers, for example, there is often a sense of shared responsibility, with children working at part-time jobs, earning their own spending money and money for clothes, even helping out with household expenses and, in many cases, actually giving their custodial parent a regular, fixed part of their earnings as "room and board."

Billy, at fifteen, is about five feet, ten inches tall; he's of medium weight, well-built, with close-cropped, curly brown hair and a very round, young, unlined face. His physical co-ordination is smooth, oiled; but he speaks with a pronounced slur and has a very small head for his body size. His manner is very open, very attentive, responsive. He handles direct, event-oriented questions well but is completely uncomprehending of anything bordering on the abstract. He is mildly retarded and—a sign of the closeness of his large family—no one in the home mentioned the fact to me prior to the taped conversation. The home is a split-level bungalow in a working-class suburb of an upstate city north of New York.

It was a hot summer evening when we talked, and the street outside was alive with children, bicycles, men in their undershirts watering their lawns or washing their cars, women and older children sitting on their front steps talking quietly, some of them drinking beer from the bottle. They were mostly contract-built homes, all similar in design, but with a small porch added here, a car-port there, to add individuality. Hi-fi amplifiers blared from a couple of nearby houses; a group of young men lounged around a large new motorcycle in one driveway with a quiet air of great expertise. When I parked my car at Billy's house children and adults alike stared with open curiosity; I was sure the whole block would know the nature of my visit before I'd completed the first tape.

"My Dad left. But he bought a lot of stuff before he left . . . We had a dishwasher and furniture he bought, but he didn't pay. And then they said they'd come and take the furniture away. So Mom had to pay. But she didn't have no money.

"My Mom, she didn't work. But she works now, and we've got the furniture back. Some of it. And some new stuff. The rest of us work, too. We do the papers, take them around every day. And we give Mom the money for groceries. My sisters, two of my sisters, they pay rent to Mom. They work all the time. But I still go to school. The rest of us do. We just do the papers. Or cut the grass for people. And give Mom the money."

Georgina, eighteen, and her sister Lisa pay that regular rent to help maintain Billy's home. Like all the other members of this family, excepting the mother, who was withdrawn and taciturn, Georgina is highly talkative. She is about five feet four inches tall, maybe 120 pounds, with bronze skin, shoulder-length brown hair and brown eyes. She wore a dark blue jersey and jeans, was barefoot, and gave an appearance of great energy and purpose-fulness. Unlike her brothers and sisters, when Georgina first sat to be interviewed she chose a chair too far away for me to reach her comfortably with the microphone; when she moved closer she sat so as to present me with only her left profile, one leg curled beneath her, rarely turning to face me fully, and smoked nervously throughout our talk. She was very attractive, exuding an aura of healthy sexuality.

"I know I changed a bit, right at the beginning. Mom was having a hard time and didn't know which way things were going, for money. So I got a job that summer, right away, in an apple orchard, picking apples, so I could be independent—and could help Mom. I was fifteen and I think I grew up a bit that way, and got closer to my family. We all tried to help each other, and help Mom.

"I guess it still affects me, the money thing. I've had a boyfriend for about three years and he wants to get engaged; he already has a ring and everything, but I won't take it. And I really think it's because of what happened to my mother. I don't want to get stuck like she did, with eight kids and him just out.

"And supposing I was twenty-two, with three kids. We'd be in an apartment, and I'd end up gettng kicked out in three months because I didn't have the rent. So I think I'll wait ten, maybe fifteen years to get married, if I get married at all. I've learned something: that is, I have to be independent, not lean on anyone for anything, no matter what happens.

"I've worked bloody hard, and now I've been made the manager of this department at the store, and I'm only eighteen. So I'm doing OK right now. I used to think at the back of my mind that maybe I'd like to get married but now it's coming into my mind that maybe I won't at all—like, forget it! Because you really have to depend on that person so much, and, if anyone changes, you have to go your own way. It's not that I think I can't handle it, but what do you do? If you've got a really small child and you have to go to work, then you have to get a baby-sitter all day—and then maybe it doesn't get properly fed or something . . . I'm a real worry-wart that way.

"I'd have to have quite a bit of money, myself, before I got married. I'd need to have something to fall back on. As soon as they told me they were going to split, I straightaway thought, 'What is she going to do for money? She doesn't work.'"

Many custodial mothers take new jobs, responsibility, income and are proud of the fact. But I also came across instances where a working mother had left her job after a separation, relying entirely on the absent father for full support. One gets contradictory reasons for this sort of change. One mother told me: "I quit my job because, as a single parent, I felt I had to have more time to devote to my children, to be sure they got as much love and attention as they'll need, now, with their father gone."

That lady's fifteen-year-old son, Tony, said:

"I kind of think maybe she quit her job because then she knew she could stick Dad for more money; and maybe that was kind of a good way for her to get her revenge—'cause he left her.

"Once when she got her cheque from him she said to me that he wouldn't be able to run around very much and just have a good time like he thought he'd be able to, 'cause he had to work a lot to get the money for us. So it was almost like she was still controlling him, still telling him what to do, even though he wasn't there any more. I think that's kind of mean. And it's not too good for anybody, because this way he's hardly got any money, he just lives in one crummy little room, downtown. And we're always short, too—not like when she was working. So who does it help?"

Here's Jack, at a disillusioned seventeen:

"One problem is that people get angry about the money, and they lie about it. And that's bad.

"For instance, I was reading this paper: it wasn't a separation agreement, it was some kind of report from a lady who came to interview us, after Dad left. I think she was a social worker, or something. I found it in a drawer when I was looking for my birth certificate for moving to a new school.

"It had stuff in it my Mom had said and things my Dad had said to the lady. I really didn't like some of the things Dad had said about my mother. For instance, he had said that she wasn't feeding us properly and clothing us properly, when it was really his fault. Because it said right there, in the report, that he was only giving my Mom thirty-five dollars a week, for the three of us, and she didn't have a job, either. But he was going out a lot, and giving things to his new girl-friends."

Angela, aged seventeen: "We never talked much about money when I was younger but then things got very tight after the split. My Mom has given us full support, has worked hard to support us, but he has never contributed the right way, the way a father should.

"It sure made me realize that maybe he really doesn't care about us, about our well-being, I mean. And he's a doctor, he's well-off, you know. It's like he thinks we're just some kind of expense, and it bothers me.

"These last years, I've seen my Mom really breaking her back, working to raise us, just to give us the things we need. We've, like, we've got more than enough, we haven't really suffered, but that's not the point; *Mom* has, by having to work so hard; and there's sure never any extra.

"But, dammit, he's a well-off man. I'm not saying that money and material things can made up for all the love and emotional things that you miss when you're younger. But it has just made me feel like I was just, just a burden to him. I don't know, I think maybe he just wanted to get even with my mother, because she didn't need him any more. Yeah. Maybe that was it. But it hurt us all. And it still really bugs me."

Literal financial desertion is infinitely more common than I'd have supposed. About one-third of the kids I interviewed lived with mothers who were getting no support whatsoever from absent fathers. Yet many of these fathers, earning decent incomes, still thought of themselves as reasonable parents, visiting their child with no evident sense of embarrassment or shame. Rosemary is sixteen:

"My Dad moved to Toronto, from Edmonton, after they separated. And he phoned my kid brother a couple of times, and said he should come to Toronto for a holiday at Easter, and in the summer. My little brother got all excited, he's only nine. But then my Mom was supposed to pay for the plane ticket and she didn't have any money, and he couldn't go. I think that was cruel; by my Dad, I mean. He even phones collect, when he calls us to wish us happy birthday."

Mac is sixteen, too. He lived in San Francisco when his parents were together:

"The first thing we found out, when Dad split, was that he hadn't been paying the mortgage on the house. The sheriff came and threw us out, but my Mom found out and we moved out some of the furniture first. We took her car, a Volkswagen, and hid it at a friend's place, because once Dad came back, with some hippy friends and he tried to take her car, and I climbed on the roof and he was driving down the street with me on the roof, hollering at him that we needed the car, until he stopped and went away. And my Mom drove it home.

"So then we borrowed some money, and sold the furniture we had taken out of the house, and we came back here, to Chicago, to live with my Mom's sister and her husband. It's pretty crowded, with seven kids altogether, and three adults, and just five rooms. And my Mom had to go on welfare. My Dad came to see us a couple of times, and he tried to borrow money from my uncle, and from my Mom.

"And my Dad's parents, they live about a mile away. They are ashamed of us, because we live on welfare. But they never ask us over or do anything to help Mom. On my birthday they sent me a card with a cheque in it; for five dollars. I tore it up.

"It was a long drive back here, in the Volkswagen, with the three of us kids. But we're better off without him, I think. He always used to have big parties, when we had the house, and wear a tuxedo and hire a bartender, and everything. But who needs all that? I have a job now, in a service station. Next year I think I'll quit school and see if I can get a job up north, where the pay is really good. Maybe in Alaska. Mom would be better off if we all got out and she just had herself to worry about. And he won't ever be any help. He's just interested in smoking pot and having a good time and running around the country with his crazy friends."

In contrast here's Hal, whom we first met on p. 34. His lifestyle seems very comfortable after five years separation; he still lives, with his mother and seven-year-old sister Wanda, in a very opulent, three-storey home on Long Island. There is a forty-foot sculpted swimming pool in the landscaped backyard. I saw three coloured TV sets between the front door and the kitchen, where we talked: one in the living-room, one in a den off the front hall, one in the kitchen itself. As we began to talk, Hal's mother entered the kitchen, punched out a number on the white phone, settled her ample bottom on a bar stool at the high counter/divider and began, without preamble, to interrupt our taped conversation:

"Is that you? So where's the damn cheque?... What do you mean you brought it out? It's not here... In the garage?... Why in hell would you leave it in the garage?... All right. Just a minute." (She replaced the phone, left the kitchen, returned in a moment, opened and poured a beer she took from the large fridge and picked up the phone again.) "Okay... Yes, okay. It's here... All right. So what about Wanda's teeth?... No, I mean the caps... Well, call me tomorrow then. And none of that crap about messages through your secretary. Okay. Bye."

She hung up, drank more beer, tossed a bag of doughnuts she had brought in from the car to Hal. He fielded the white bag, one-handed, and she left the room again, without speaking. In a moment I heard her in the front hall, a radio playing loudly and a vacuum cleaner roaring as we continued our talk.

Hal is unlike his mother—dark where she is blonde; slim and quiet where she seems heavy and ponderous; relaxed, casual, open where she appears watchful, abrupt, peremptory. He has soft bangs fringing his forehead and was wearing a football T-shirt, jeans, and sneakers without socks:

"The hardest thing for me about being divorced is that my Dad really hates it when he gets any bills, and so they still argue a lot; all the time, just about. When my Mom's boy-friend, Jack, lived here, he broke our hi-fi and so Mom ordered a new one. And Dad didn't think he should be buying hi-fi's for Jack, right?

"And Dad says all the bills have always been too high, since they separated, about four years ago. But they're a bit lower, now. We're not using so much heat, and we have to keep the pool heater turned down now, most of the time, except if Mom is having a party. And we don't use the lights in the pool now, hardly ever. I guess, before Dad left, we had a lot more money. But now, there's the two places to look after, so there just isn't as much left to go around.

"The biggest difference, for me, is that before we had a man come in to do the pool and a man come in to do the gardening. Now, with two houses to keep, there isn't so much money, and so I have to clean the pool. And I do a lot of the gardening. It takes quite a while; about an hour or two, almost every day, to do it all."

For those less well off, hope springs eternal. Let's close this chapter with Alec, almost seven.

"We had to sell our house. Mom did. And we moved to this place. I like it. I've got lots of friends here. There are really a lot of kids in the development, all over the place.

"When Daddy pays Mom, every week, she buys tickets for the lottery. And we sit down, in the kitchen, and we always make a list of all the stuff we're going to buy when she wins. She said she's going to buy a yacht, that's a really big sailboat, and a real big house. When we win the lottery. Or when Grandma dies, because she's got a lot of money, and Mommy will get it all. But I think we'll win with a ticket. Because I like my Grandma."

6
Self-reliance

We've looked at three areas of adaptation. Now we can start to ask how the children emerge from the process.

The most common myth which divorced parents use to reassure themselves and their friends is: "There's never been any pressure on the children. No matter what difficulties there've been between us we've both made certain we didn't take it out on the kids, or force them to accept responsibilities or grow up before their time. *We've always made sure they understood this wasn't their problem.*"

Let's start by looking at this "lack of pressure" at work on two children: Hank and Jack.

Hank was fourteen when his mother decided to move from Denver to England; she'd never been to England, but, two years after her divorce, a surgical fresh start seemed indicated. One older daughter had opted, the year before, to move three hundred miles and live with her father; an older son was, at nineteen, finished school, working, living in an apartment with two friends. Hank had two younger siblings, a girl and boy, eight and ten years old. He is a quiet young man, self-possessed, articulate, comfortable in his skin. His voice is soft, non-assertive, his manner direct, matter-of-fact:

"When Mom decided to move to England I figured it was partly, maybe, to spite Dad. I mean he couldn't afford to visit us or have us to visit him very often if she did that; not more than once a year, for sure.

"She really organized everything; she sold the house and sold or gave away a lot of our stuff; I really missed some of it—skis and things like that. And she and Dad agreed we could each decide, any of us who were twelve or older, whether we wanted to go to England or stay in the States. The two younger ones, they agreed, were to go with her.

"So I had to decide. I didn't really want to move; I had all my friends and everything in Denver and I didn't want to be that far from my Dad. And I had my college picked out and all.

"But I said I'd go. I went camping, in the mountains, with my Dad that summer, just before we were supposed to go; for about a month. And I told him I was going. I figured the younger kids needed somebody older, some male, around the house, to help them, to fix things; whatever. I didn't think it'd be good for them, just living with Mom. And I figured, when I finished school, in four years, I could come home to go to college—they'd be older then.

"So that's what I decided. I mean, Dad wasn't going to be there so it was really up to me. I didn't really resent that, he couldn't do anything about it; but I really didn't want to go."

No responsibilities?

Jack is seventeen, rangy, with stiff, wiry hair springing out from his scalp; his hands seem too large even for his six-foot frame and his face, arms, hands are heavily freckled. His tone is objective, analytical; he sounds a bit like a Martian sociologist describing the fate of alien strangers rather than like an intimate participant in the events he discussed:

"I guess Helen and May (his younger sisters) were a little younger so they wanted to stay with their mother, eh? Jean was older than me, two years older, and she was working already, so we stayed with the father, eh? I was given a choice; they both said so.

"Mom said, 'If you want to go with me, it's OK. If you want to go with your father it's OK.' And I just—I chose to go with my father; I figured it would be better for me, I can't really think why, now. I had reasons, you know, summing it up either way. Well, where we were moving it was closer for me to go to school; well—well, no, it was about the same, actually.

"It was a hard decision, which way to go. But I knew that the two smaller ones were going with the mother, eh? So—so, I decided to go with the father.

"I mean—well, I thought he needed some company, too. He was pretty low, eh?—pretty down. So I went with him."

/ This forced maturity runs parallel with a theme that was clear and ever-present at some point and in some form in virtually all of my taped conversations: self-reliance. Paraphrased: "You can't count on anybody else so you'd better become independent and make sure you can stand alone." On the positive side, several children saw such self-reliance as the key benefit they had derived from the divorce.

Joe is thirteen, fair, forthright, almost aggressive:

"I can tell you one thing; it's really smartened me up. I mean, it's really helped me; in school, everywhere. You find out, don't you? This kind of stuff could happen to anybody. So you watch out. You sure don't want stuff like that to happen to you ever again, do you? So you learn to be careful. You smarten up—or else.

"I've got some friends who are divorced. But we don't talk about it. It's enough already. Who needs to talk about it anyway? It's a sad thing. Some people, other people, I mean, some of my friends, feel sad if we talk about it. So we don't.

"But I've sure wisened-up to things; to life. That's why I don't talk about it. I just get sad that the marriage didn't work out. And I miss having somebody to talk to when you need him. 'Cause my mother's never around and anyway she's busy with her stuff. But when I have my problems there's nobody to talk with about them.

"But it doesn't matter. I don't like to talk about it anyhow, I've wisened-up."

Andrea is eight; she is slim, dark, assertive, a trifle antagonistic during our conversation.

"It didn't affect me. I don't know nothing about it. It hasn't got anything to do with me. I'm the same. Mommy's different; she cries a lot but I stay away when she's crying. It's just made me smarter. I'm smarter now. I'm careful. Other kids have to be nice to me. If we're not going to play, I decide. That's 'cause I'm smarter. I've gotten intelligenter; I play with smart kids like me;

not with my brother; he worries about it too much. Not like me."

Kerry is nineteen: "You have to face it; we all do. We're the products of our parents. I am. My sister is very suspicious; ever since the divorce, four years ago, she's suspicious of everybody; so is my mother; and we're the result of our parents, too. But I'm my own person, mostly, thank goodness.

"For the longest time, I guess until this summer, I couldn't seem to get along with anybody, keep a friendship. I was suspicious, you know, like my mother; like my older sister.

"But I'm OK now. You have to just be your own person. I'm like that. Now I am. It doesn't seem to have affected me in how I relate to other people. Not any more. I don't think so. I hope not. But I think I'm OK now. Not like my Mom. Or my sister.

"Well, look. I was a very angry child, a very angry teenager. I really felt isolated, being the next-to-the-oldest one. So I think I became very independent at an early age—an earlier age because of that. I mean, I didn't want to be like my Mom, always suspicious; and I didn't want to be like my Dad—never on time, never dependable about money or anything. So it was better to just be independent. Right?

"So, I think it's put me in good standing. I mean, I wouldn't want to go through it again, or anything like that. But I don't think it's really hurt me; maybe even helped. I think I was a very reserved person—when it first happened—for a few years, a real introvert. Not like now at all. You wouldn't have recognized me then."

We met Angela on p. 76. She's seventeen, tense, pretty, articulate, candid:

"When you go to a friend's house, you know, and see how they live, like with a father, and all those different things—then you sort of think, 'Well, something's missing. We don't have that sort of thing at home.'

"I have a hard time expressing love. Well, to the opposite sex at least. With men I can't—you know, express my feelings. I mean, it's having a serious effect on me right now, and I'm only seventeen. I'm paranoid; I'm very scared of being rejected or hurt. You know it's just—there's just—I'm—I'm scared to show someone how I feel. Because I'm scared that, if I tell them, that they're going to use it to hurt me.

"I feel deprived of—well, just a fatherly love. You know. I've never had it, can't remember it. So you try to make up for it in other ways and you try to be more independent, to stand alone more. But you can't make it up with other people, somehow—can't let go enough. And being alone, that's not very good, is it?

"But I'm definitely better off now. I'm sure I am. If I'd gone with my father, I mean, instead of my mother, I'm sure I would be a very cold person. And I would never have known enough, in my head, to start working these problems out now.

"I mean, when you figure it out, most children stay at home until they're eighteen or twenty, on average, unless they get married or something. So they don't have to think for themselves so much as I do; I mean, I wouldn't have known any different, and if my parents had stayed together, who knows what would have happened?

"I've got a lot more self-confidence now. I'd never have had that. Not if they'd stayed together.

"I think I could still use help. With the problems I've still got. Even—even to talk; maybe to talk to somebody, even, that you don't know. So you could—you could just, just lay it out on a table. You know, all your feelings, and you could work from there.

"It's hard. It's really hard. Thinking about some of those things too, because—well, you wonder: 'What am I gonna do? Am I gonna be like this for the rest of my life?'

"Those feelings are haunting. And you know, there's nothing you can do about it at the time. And so you push it away. And like all problems, they come back. Those haunting thoughts."

The most haunting of all thoughts for divorced kids is clearly the fear that the marital errors of their parents may turn out to be a fate rather than a lesson, in which case their accelerated maturity will engender cynicism or apathy rather than self-reliance and wisdom.

None of that is necessary, of course. If "forced growth" is a mixed blessing it can, with some loving attention, lead to positive ends, to feelings of accomplishment rather than perceptions of loss. My personal conviction is that my own children are more self-reliant, more positive and responsible human beings than would have been the case without their experience of parental separation; but I don't think them less sensitive to others.

Equally, I'm aware of many lost opportunities when I could have talked with them about their needs to adapt to circumstance, their feelings about marital love, the chance in their lives for emotional fulfilment in adult years.

I was, with my own children, slow in understanding that it's probably more than just OK to let them be aware of a new emotional attachment in the life of a divorced parent; it may be essential. As they see and accept that a parent who saw one adult relationship dissolve is, nonetheless, still fully capable of adult love, they may hope more for themselves.

PART THREE
Parents and Kids

7
Parents

We've been looking at how children adapt. But what about their parents? In the next three chapters divorced kids describe their current views of and relations with their mothers and fathers. Sometimes, of course, their words are illustrative of the pressures felt by *all* youngsters. Many teenage girls have trouble communicating with their mothers, for example. But divorced kids blame the marital split for their problems; that is *their* reality.

It's been my experience with my own children that they are usually reticent about discussing their mother with me. And my interviews suggested that virtually all divorced kids are loath to discuss one parent with the other. Beyond the childish games played by parents in keeping secrets from one another, and binding their children to secrecy as well, there is a natural protective instinct in these kids—a desire to keep their separate lives with each parent watertight, safe from the hurricanes of ugly emotion that made their lives so turbulent when both were together. The kids don't want any more of that, if they can help it; and so they tend to behave like good little double agents, with evasion or dreamy silence, when asked even commonplace and non-threatening questions by one parent about the other. These kids are even more reluctant ever to say anything which might offend the parent they are with—so very often neither parent gets a true picture of their feelings.

I believe my "travelling bartender" role helped me to go behind this reticence. Certainly I was surprised by the perception and psychological shrewdness of the replies. While the complexity of parent/children relationships was evident in the wide variety of comments, nevertheless some patterns did seem to be present, and we'll examine these in Part Four.

Let's start with mothers. Linda, at twelve, describes the change most commonly recognized by children during the first twelve to eighteen months of separation.

"Mom isn't depressed all the time, now. She used to be crying all the time, upstairs in her room, before they separated; and even after. But she gets out more now. I guess, now, she has made a life for herself. She seems to be quite a bit happier now."

It's not a surprising metamorphosis, but it's interesting to see just how often the children elaborate on it.

Lisa, at twenty: "She's a much more interesting person, now. I think that while she was married, and the marriage wasn't working out, she was just sort of living on a day-to-day basis. Now she's a totally different person. She's found out there's more to life than just being around the house and the kids. She really takes a special interest in herself, in how she looks. She goes out now, quite a bit; she works—that's good for her. She even goes to a dance club, once a week; that's certainly not my old, conservative-type mother. She even has her hair styled, now; before, she'd just get it cut once in a while, not even have it shampooed at the beauty parlour—she'd just have it cut, wash it herself and maybe stick it in rollers. What a change!"

Wesley is eight: "She won't ever talk about it; just says it wasn't any good with Dad. I guess it wasn't, 'cause she laughs a lot more, now. She has a lot more fun with her friends, and we do more interesting stuff now; she has more time with us. I think it's best to live with Mom; she takes a lot better care of us. When my sister and I go to my Dad's place, we always have to wash all his dishes. He just lets them pile up in the sink and there aren't any dishes to eat with until we wash them. And we have to clean out the fridge; there's all this rotten cheese and stuff in it.

"Here it's always nice and clean; clean dishes and everything. Also, here, I get to live in a big house with my Mom—and Dad just has one floor of a house and it's kind of small.

"But I don't think she'll get married any more. She says she just wants to be with us, now. Nobody else."

Wilma, at seventeen: "At first, last year, when they separated, my Mom used to put my Dad down quite a bit, after he left. And I really didn't like that very much. It didn't seem fair, just hearing one side of it all the time. And it was no fun being with her, when she was just complaining about him. But now she doesn't do that so much.

"The biggest difference is that it seems warmer here, now. I mean, before he left, it wasn't fights, really, it was just a kind of coldness towards each other; the whole house seemed cold, especially for instance, when we were all eating together. Now, with her not complaining so much, we can sometimes enjoy each other's company.

"Certainly mother is a lot easier to get along with, now. We don't fight as much. Maybe that's partly 'cause I'm a year older, too; but I think she is definitely a much happier person."

Janet's mother has gone to work since the divorce. Like most children, Janet sees this as a positive thing: "Since Mommy got a job she's a lot prettier. She got skinnier, and she changed her hair, it's kind of red, now. And she brings home treats, on payday."

But there can be negatives, too. William, who is thirteen:

"Well, sometimes it's good that Mom works now; and sometimes it's not so good. It brings more money into the house, and that's good. But, boy! It sure makes her grouchy sometimes; she just comes home and complains about her boss and she is all tired and grouchy. And she doesn't have so much time to bake any more, and stuff like that. Mostly, once in a while, we get that junky stuff from the bakery. Or she'll bring home some doughnuts."

For Andrew, at fourteen, it's a good thing that his mother left her job:

"I didn't used to know her very well; she was always working, and then working at home when she was here. She'd come home really tired, and, well, I didn't feel very comfortable with her. I felt a lot more comfortable with my Dad, because we'd do things together more. So I was worried when I found out I was living alone with just her.

"But now I've gotten to know her better, because she's home just about all the time now. She's doing little bits of things here and there, but mostly she's at home. And we've done some stuff together, like growing these plants that don't have any dirt or soil, and experimenting. And I've kind of gotten to like her more, now."

Not every parental relationship improves after separation, though it should be obvious by now that very many do. One set of lingering effects for divorced kids results from the absence of male, adult role models—results, too, from role models whose own values and behaviour patterns have been skewed by post-separation trauma, or from confused impressions of existing models:

Farley, at nine years of age, is a veteran truant; he lived in a public housing development with his mother for the three years after her separation and divorce, was in frequent minor scrapes with the police, participated in several acts of petty theft and vandalism with other children. On a psychologist's advice, he is living, for a while, in a "group home," where trained surrogate parents supervise a half-dozen "problem" children.

"Well, I used to tell my Mom, 'Why should I go to school? You quit in grade six so you've done OK.' And then she'd yell at me and get mad. And I'd say I didn't think school was any good and she'd tell me I would never get a job. And I'd say I didn't care, she didn't have any job after Dad left, and I could live on welfare like she did. So she sent me here, and now I have to do homework every night and get up at six-thirty and stuff. But she still doesn't have no job. So I don't know."

Paul, seven: "My Mom is different now; not so happy—more angry all the time. She still talks about my Dad a lot, all of the time. But now, she always calls him 'Your father.' That's all she calls him. I think she's mad and sad at him. So she's mad and sad at us, too, most of the time. She does more work, now. And she's got longer hair. She's really thin, now. She used to be fat."

Barry, fourteen, lives in a small rented house with his mother and two younger sisters; he is extremely tense and radiates a feeling of anger:

"They split when I was about seven, so I'm not really sure what she was like, before; I can remember a little bit. They both used to drink a lot, I know that; and have really big fights. She doesn't drink now; but she seems tired all the time and she gets mad a lot.

"She told me that the marriage was never any good. She said it just was bad from the first day, and that it kept getting worse after that. And I don't think she wanted us much; it's as if she resents having us—she'd be happier if we weren't all here. But what I want to know is, why did they get married in the first place if they didn't like each other? They sure didn't do us any big favours. I think she's tired of me a lot, and mad at me; but how does she think I feel?"

Most children learn early to say things like, "Dad, Mom says I can have _____ if it's OK with you." They then use the reverse phrase on Mom, and often get the desired treat, have the friend sleep over at the weekend or whatever before the parents compare notes. Divorced kids have an advantage because of the fragmented and desultory nature of most communication between their parents; many of them learn to play this particular game rather well.

So did Annette. Annette is eight; her pigtails (braids) are auburn, her eyes hazel, her forehead high and round, and freckled. She is a nervous child, not self-possessed, not, one felt, very secure. At age seven, a year after "her" divorce, as she calls it, she even progressed to childish blackmail. She could always go and live with Daddy, after all, she'd remind her mother when thwarted in some small request. But Mom had some weapons, too. They were heavy artillery compared with Annette's pop-guns:

"One day I told Mommy I'd go and stay with my Dad if I couldn't have something. I knew I couldn't. I was only teasing. But she said, 'OK.'

"And then she took all my clothes off. And then she put me on the front porch, where everybody could see me. And then she locked the door so I couldn't get in the house.

"Then she hollered through the door. She said, 'That's how your father gave you to me and that's how you can go back to him. Go ahead.'

"But I couldn't. Then she let me in after I cried for a while. And she said she'd do it again. If I ever said it again. So I don't. Say it, I mean. I was really scared. And my friends saw me. They laughed at me."

Annette's mother has been known to brag of her salutary therapy to friends. It should happen to her.

Diane lives in an opulent home in Detroit; she is seventeen, with two older sisters, has just over one year's experience of living alone with her mother:

"My Mom has changed a bit; she tries to be nicer, sometimes. But she wouldn't care if I went to live with my Dad. I think she'd just like to have the whole house to herself—my sisters away at school and me with him. She's mean; she won't let me do the things I want to do.

"She goes out with other men, sometimes. It doesn't bother me. The most bother is the way she's always talking about money. Like, she doesn't seem to realize that my Dad has to pay for his place, too, and he had to buy furniture and everything. And he pays for our house, and one of my sisters is going to college and now Mom is going to send my other sister to a school in France, and she's even talking about getting another car. She just doesn't seem to have any sense about money.

"Maybe it would be better if she got married again. She likes to have somebody, a man, to look after; and she likes young children—it would be good, maybe, if she married a man with some young children."

Diane stroked her longish hair with her left hand, combing the strands through her fingers, looked rather fiercely into the middle distance, and added, in a rush of words: "But one thing: my Mom really likes to dominate everything and everybody. So I think it wouldn't work, if she got married again, unless she married the kind of a man who is stronger than she is. She should have the kind of man who could stand up to her."

On the subject of men Alma, who's fifteen, is learning from her mother.

"Mom says you shouldn't trust any men. You should just get them to give you a good time. That's what she does now—like she really goes out a lot now, with all different men. And she makes them take her to really nice places, restaurants and things, and they give her presents. One took her to New York for last weekend.

"Mom says you should just get what you can from them; 'cause that's all they want, too. To get whatever they can from you. So why not? I think she's right. Just get whatever you can."

Relatively few children spoke about a new-found and more relaxed lifestyle on the part of their fathers, though since the majority of the children I interviewed were living with their mothers it's possible they might have known less about their father's "private" life.

There were some exceptions, however. Here's one which again raises the question of role models.

Angus, fourteen: "My Dad told me he got married too young. And he didn't have any fun before, he was too busy working and supporting Mom and only being with her. And life was a bore.

"Now he goes out all the time; and he's got nicer clothes and a sports car. And he goes to a lot of parties.

"He has a ball now. I'm not going to make the mistakes he did. I'm going to have fun while I'm young. I'm starting already, I mean, I have a beer once in a while; and I go to more parties; stuff like that."

Jim, also fourteen, said of his father "He's a little more wild now—he's gotten sort of younger."

Views of fathers, especially among children living with their mother, tend to polarize; some children feel estrangement, but others say that the divorce has allowed them to be closer.

The crucial time, for most children, is the "visit," potentially a time of great pleasure, all too often an uncomfortable or nerve-wracking event. It's worth remembering that the children we're about to hear from are talking about fathers who have probably thought rather well of themselves, supposed they gave their children no pain, never imagined themselves an object of the intense scrutiny, and, often, pity, of their divorced kids.

Amanda is nineteen: "Dad has changed; he's not really well and he's had to slow down. I know if he could do it all over again it would be differently, or so he says, anyway. I know he regrets a lot of the things he's said and done and I know he is a very lonely person.

"I go to see him when I can but it's really emotional. He worries so much about us, it's really amazing. Someone's only got to sniffle and he's right up there, ready for a coronary attack.

"So we tend, all of us, to shelter him. He's not your most liberal person; he's East European, and very strict. So we tend to shelter him from the roaring Seventies.

"I think that my mother got the better of the whole deal. After all, she has us—for company—and she got the house, and friends stayed mostly with her. My Dad was always a loner; anyway, you don't need company to get drunk. But now that he's had time to think about it I think he realizes that it's probably for the best. But he's a very lonely man, I think."

Susan, sixteen: "Dad's a lot quieter now. He doesn't talk as much. He's sort of careful with us; with all three of us. I think maybe he's afraid we'll turn against him, not want to see him, if he talks too much.

"I feel quite a bit further away from him now, because he's not here—and so we can't talk to him. I mean, if you do well in a test at school, when you come home you can't tell him, because he isn't here. And I don't call him; my brother does; maybe it's easier for a boy. I don't know if I'd have anything to say; I don't know if he'd be interested. I guess I just don't want to bother him, to just tell him about a test, or something.

"I don't think he's any happier. He seems kind of lonely now. It's a bit hard to talk to him . . . Usually when I see him, we go out to dinner and stuff like that. So then, if there's nothing to talk about, well at least there's something to do. I don't think we could sit around in his apartment and talk."

Angela, seventeen (see p. 84): "When I was younger I used to think I had to try really hard to see my Dad a lot, to maintain the relationship with him, you know. I was eleven then, when they separated. And you really try, especially at first, because you miss so many things—you know, like Christmas and birthdays.

"But sooner or later you realize, I realized, that the way he was—like, I couldn't change him or even make him into somebody I could be comfortable with. I could never really talk to him about anything important. There's just this big communications gap.

"It's a very big gap—and, the things I feel—I just can't say to him . . . There's no—it's very easy to express love. And he can't seem to express love. And that's really made an effect on me, trying to deal with him—or with anybody, for that matter.

"I really needed to be reassured, you know, after they separated. But he never gave that, never could give that; not in the way that you really needed it. He didn't even seem to know just how to give a little pat on back, just to make you feel good, to help you feel better, if maybe you did something good. He always set such high goals for me that I felt they were impossible; and even if I did that, if I reached them, then he'd still probably say, 'Well, you could have done a little better.'

"So I had to decide, well, who am I living for, anyway? Him or me? So now I don't expect anything from him. It'd be nice, though, if he noticed good things I do, just once in a while."

Barbara, seventeen: "I was seven when they separated, and it was pretty hard to understand why he left. So it really changed my feelings towards him, because I was always so tense when he'd come over to get me. I'd just end up crying, almost every time. I wasn't the same with him at all as with my mother because I just didn't know him; he was like a stranger.

"And he'd always be late; by the time he got there I'd be so worked up I couldn't speak, couldn't talk to him or anything, just nod my head. He'd say he was going to come at ten in the morning, and I'd wake up about five, as if it was Christmas or something. And then he maybe wouldn't come until about three; by then I was just exhausted, from waiting. Then, to make up for it, he'd probably keep me late; and I'd be so tired, from the strain and everything,

I'd just want to get home, get into my own bed."

For Angus, though, things are improving:

"I see him pretty often, about as often as I want to; I didn't used to, but it's better now. Actually, I used to see him once a week, on a sort of schedule; now I see him about every three weeks—but now it's more when we both want to.

"He didn't use to invite me to stay over, and I couldn't invite myself; I think there was this girl there, or something. But now, he's living with this lady, and he's started to invite me to stay over and it's better."

Frank is not so lucky. At sixteen, he is slim, wiry, fair-haired, blue-eyed. He is engaging, open, full of vitality and enthusiasm. About a year after his parents' separation Frank was in a serious auto accident. One arm and one leg were seriously injured. For a month, heavily infected, Frank hovered between life and death, subjected to repeated surgery and kept sane by regular doses of morphia; then his arm was amputated.

In the first four weeks Frank's father, working in a city two hour's drive from the Birmingham hospital where he lay, came once to visit; he stayed about ten minutes.

Two days before the amputation, about which he felt considerable and justifiable trepidation, Frank telephoned his father, "just to talk." Still heavily sedated for pain, Frank asked his father why a loved pet had been "put away" at his father's insistence shortly before the marital break:

"Dad got really mad. He hollered at me and told me to stop interfering, and said it was none of my business, that he'd already explained.

"Then he told me he wasn't going to come and see me any more if that was how I was going to behave. He said my mother could look after me, anyway. He said I was ungrateful and I didn't deserve to have him come and see me.

"Then he slammed the phone down.

"I guess he meant it. He hasn't called or written. Or come to see me. Maybe he doesn't want to see me. Like this, I mean."

It would be too easy to say Frank is likely better off without that father. Frank doesn't think so.

Finally, two rather more reflective comments. In each instance there's been a dispute over custody.

Roger, twelve: "My Dad started a fight, to get me, with lawyers and everything—but mostly I think he just wanted my brother, my older brother, 'cause they are a lot closer than him and me. The lawyer talked to my brother, but they made me stay outside; I didn't get to talk to the lawyer. My brother said he didn't want to go—he wanted to stay with my Mom and me. So that was the end of that. But I can still talk to him and everything; when I see him, I mean."

And Hal, ten: "My Dad was trying to get us to live with him. He tells us it was my Mom's fault, when they separated. Sometimes I think it was my Dad's fault and sometimes I think it was Mom's. After they have arguments, still, sometimes I'll talk to my Dad and he'll prove one point; and then I'll talk to my Mom, and she'll prove another point. So I don't know.

"I know my Dad is still trying to get us to live with him. He's not trying as hard now, though, I think he's trying slowly now, so there won't be arguments.

"I don't really care where we live, with my Mom or my Dad. My Dad takes better care of us; he takes better care of my clothes, of our clothes. I know that's one reason he wants to live with us—he always has to wash our clothes, when we go to visit him. He always says they're filthy. But if I live with my Dad I can visit my Mom; and if I live with my Mom, like now, I can visit my Dad; I really see as much of my Dad as I do of my Mom.

"I guess it really doesn't matter which one you live with, if you can just be friends with them both."

It's clear that even when relations with a father have improved, "visits" can be uneasy.

My proudest boast and most comforting rationale, thinking of my relationship with my own children, always used to be that, while we might be together less now, the time we spent was "concentrated," spent entirely in doing things together, being together. Beyond that, I'd "taken pains," as I thought, to separate any of my strains or conflicts with their mothers from our time together as father and child. I was wrong, on both counts.

First, the "concentrated time" about which I'd been so self-righteous was often marred, for the kids, by pressures of work, by the fact that we were together in the wrong ways and places—too often public, commercial places, where we were just a few among the throng, not properly "together." Also I'd failed to understand fully that individual kids need time alone with each parent, as individuals, not always as a "group." Parental visits tend to be for all of the children at the same time; so all the kids miss out on the one-for-one talks and times that permit real airing of things that matter to the kids. Worse, many parents tend to spend what little individual time they do allocate or arrange with only and always the eldest child—or the eldest child of their own sex. Little boys in their father's custody tend to complain that, "Mom always spends more time talking to my big sister, when we see her. She doesn't do as much stuff with me." Little girls living with their mothers have the mirror image of that problem, when Dad takes the boys on a canoe trip and leaves the girls with his new wife or lover.

It's abundantly clear to me, now, that all children, like all adults, need individual attention. Not just the eldest; not just the boys; or just the girls. Remembering that the statistically-average divorce involves three-plus kids, it's easier to understand that it may be in this area that most absentee parents, mothers and fathers, fail most abysmally.

When a parent does take the pains, on occasion, to have the children for individual visits, the results can make for a dramatic improvement.

I had one other hole in my smug perception big enough to accomodate a very large truck: children bring very heavy tangible baggage to every parental visit. Like Jacob Marley's chain of cash-boxes, ledgers and coins, it is forged of every experience they've had while with the "other" parent. These kids carry a freight, too, of awareness—for example, the knowledge that Dad's interest in the new lady in his life may very well shorten his attention span for them.

Despite this, parental relationships often improve after divorce, as we've seen; even relationships between the parents themselves may be more amiable when the strains of maintaining an unhappy marriage are removed—a change that does more for the emotional health of children than any opulent home or fat maintainance allowance.

Here, to close this chapter, is an optimistic note, a "success story." Sally, at eighteen:

"At one time, just before they broke up, I really kind of hated my mother. But now I'm really, really, close to her; and I can tell her anything at all. At one time, when I was sixteen , I told her that as soon as I could I was going to quit school, get a job and get out. But now I'm really having a good time; I've got a good job, and I pay rent here, to help out, and I don't want to leave at all.

"She has really changed, too, she's much happier, much friendlier, easier to talk to and be with. I think she's done a really good job with herself. Now she takes care of herself. I don't think she'd want to get married again. She says there are too many problems—that people change too much; and she's contented, now."

"Before, when she didn't work, she just went shopping or something. Now, she takes dancing lessons, she buys herself some decent clothes, goes out to a couple of clubs. Even the way she looks—she's careful with her hair and everything. She even got herself an Afro-cut—it blew my mind. Before she'd just watch TV. She didn't know whether it was Monday, Tuesday or Wednesday. Just sit home all day."

Her father too seems much happier. Sally's account of her relations with him contains a wealth of advice for parents:

"I like him a lot better, now that he's not here . . . I don't think he even used to notice me, when he was here. He'd step on my face to go and see my older sister, and not even notice I was there; I was just the one in the middle . . . So we used to fight a lot; because I wouldn't do what he wanted all the time. I figured I should do what I want to do, not always do what he's interested in. Like, he just wanted me to stay home and read books and wear dresses.

"But he treats me like a person, now; like a grown-up. Before he used to really get upset if I made any decisions for myself, but now we'll go and have a picnic or I'll take him to lunch sometimes; and once, on his birthday, I took him to dinner. It's like we're friends now, not like he's a father.

"I never, in my life, talked to him about any problems; I never would. But now, he asks me questions and it seems like he really means it. He cares, I think now. And I feel really good when I'm with him. Because, when he left, I can honestly say I didn't miss him. But now, I do miss him and now I'll take time out to go and see him, whereas before, when he was home, if he was here I'd make plans to do just anything so I could be out, stay away, so I wouldn't be around him; because the less I was there, when he was, the less I'd get into trouble.

"I think he's changed, in the sense that—he's always cared for the kids, always tried to make a nice Christmas for us and nice birthdays, even when money was short—and I think he feels he's lost something; and I think he's scared that if he slips up, then that's it; we don't have to go and see him any more.

"In a way, really, my Dad seems to be happier. I mean, he knows, now, we'll come to see him because we want to, not, like before, when we used to go to the park all together once a month because we had to go."

8
Spying

Being "friends" with both parents isn't so easy if you're being used as a middle-man. The espionage network operated reluctantly by divorced kids would put Sherlock Holmes's Baker Street Irregulars to shame; it might even provide instructive study for MI5, the Deuxième Bureau or the CIA. Divorced kids are the prototypical double agents, living in one camp but making regular forays into the other, carrying messages and data both ways, often subjected to mixed loyalties, often finding their "patriotism" eroded by knowledge acquired during these expeditions. And, like most double agents, they are generally "recruited" against their will, used cynically without regard for their own convictions or inclinations. They hate it. Sometimes, like the grown-up agents they ape and mirror, they come to feel hate or contempt for themselves. Usually their response is one of anger, weariness, irritation.

Sometimes the spying, with its Byzantine activities and interrogations, takes place *ante bellum*:

Linda, fourteen: "My Dad used to go away drinking every Friday night and sometimes stay away until Sunday night, just drinking and stuff. That was with these friends we used to have, but now they are just *his* friends, this man and lady.

"So, sometimes, Mom used to ask me to look in his car for stuff, after he came home, and when he was in the house. And once I found a bottle of whiskey in the car, and that was one of the times my Mom made my Dad sleep on the chesterfield, in the living-room for a while.

"Another time was when we were doing the laundry, and Mom said, 'Look in all your Dad's pockets and see what you find,' and so I looked in his suits and everything, even though we didn't wash his suits. His wallet was there—he was sleeping—and it had a card in it. My Mom was always making remarks about this card to me, and hollering at him about it. The card said, 'Meet me at this place, for lunch on Friday.' Friday mornings my Dad always used to get all dressed-up to go to work, and usually he doesn't get dressed-up for work, so then my Mom knew he'd go out with her—with this friend—at lunch time on Friday.

"That was when Mom told him—she went and woke him up—that she was leaving pretty soon. And she did."

But curiosity and antipathy directed at the "other woman" rarely end when the marriage ends:

Hal, ten (see pp. 34 and 77): "Since he left, every time my Dad comes to pick us up for a visit, an argument happens. Usually it's about his girl-friend, Jane. My Mom really didn't want to have me and my sister ever with her, with Jane; she was always asking about her. And so my Dad had to lie a lot to my Mom, like telling her that Jane wasn't there; and so we had to lie, too, because my Mom wouldn't want Wanda and I to be there, if Jane was—and then we wouldn't be able to see our Dad. So he used to tell us not to tell, but Wanda was pretty young—sometimes she'd forget, and tell.

"Once, my Mom let my Dad have a record player from the house to use at his place. For him to use when we were visiting him. And my Mom thought that was OK. But then, this time, after my Dad brought us home, my Mom was undressing my sister, to get ready for bed, and she asked if Jane was there. My sister said she was. So then we had to get right back dressed again, and my Mom said I had to take her to the apartment, show her the apartment, so she could take the record player back so my Dad and Jane couldn't use it. But my Mom didn't know where Jane's apartment was and didn't know her name or anything. So she made me get dressed and we all went in the car, to show her.

"And I could only find it if we started from my Dad's office, 'cause that's how we went—I didn't know the name of the street. So we went to my Dad's office, first. And then I knew my way, and we found the apartment building. But I didn't know which apartment it was—just one high up somewhere; it's a really big building; and I didn't know the last name. So we tried one apartment, and it was the wrong one; and we tried a couple more, but they were wrong, too. It took about an hour, or maybe two hours. Mom was really sure she was going to find that apartment—she kept asking all these questions about it. But we didn't and she gave up, and we came home and got undressed all over again.

"Now Dad lives with Jane, all the time, and they've got a baby. She's nice—she's like a mother to me. Mom doesn't seem to care quite as much now, but they still fight every time he comes for us; but I don't have to lie as much, now. That's better, 'cause my sister isn't very good at it."

Angus is thirteen: "My Mom doesn't know too much about my Dad any more. He says that's better, 'cause she used to call him a lazy bum and all stuff like that. He's moved quite a bit and she doesn't know his address, right now.

"I see him about once a week; we usually just go to a park or something like that. Then, when I come back here, she comes to me and she tries to use me as a middle-man. She's already divorced and everything, but she's still trying to get more money and stuff from him. So she'll come to me, asking 'Where's his address?', 'How much money has he got?' and things like that.

"But what I think is *she* has to solve her problems. I just think if she wants to solve her problems, okay, but I want no part of it. I don't think she should ask me that stuff, I'm no spy. All he does is ask, 'How's your Mom?' and that's it. That's how it should be."

Simon is twelve: "We see Dad every second weekend. And then, when we come home, my mother always complains that we're mean with her 'cause we don't tell her everything.

"I mean, every time we come back—every time—Mom asks us lots and lots of questions about what went on; and who was there and what did they say. And what was Dad like with the other people, and what were they doing together. And did we go anywhere; and who else came. Nothing but questions.

"And then my brother and I get bored by so much talking and everything, so much trying to remember so much. And then she gets really mad and yells at us. And then we always have a big argument, every time we come home. Because of the questions."

My own ears burned most fiercely when divorced kids raised their roles as couriers. As with most divorced couples, my wives and I have been through periods when it simply seemed too hazardous to risk direct contact, when we were apprehensive of arguments and scenes, and so resorted to written communications, on one side, or on both. There must have been a score of occasions for each of my children when I would say, off-handedly, "Oh. Give this letter to your Mom when you get home." Or they'd inform me that "There's an envelope in my suitcase, from Mommy."

Often the letter for me would be handed over only as they were leaving. Only now do I understand that the belated delivery was almost certainly because they feared my reading of the message would trigger an angry phone call or confrontation which they wanted postponed until they'd gone. Sometimes the dangerous envelope would not be handed to me at all, but simply left on my bed or my desk, where I'd find it after they'd gone. A couple of them turned up, days or weeks later, under a bed, or mixed with my soiled laundry.

Not least among the reasons these kids are inhibited about delivering such messages, verbal or written, is their clear understanding that they are often carefully guided missile weapons designed to hurt and injure the other parent.

Wilma, seventeen: "At first they would hardly ever talk to each other, ever. And so they were always saying, 'Tell her this,' or 'You can tell him that.' Lots of times it was the kind of thing that was just going to make trouble or cause a scene and so sometimes we just wouldn't deliver the message at all. But that's bad, too, because then they'd get into a big fight about something one of them was supposed to do—but they hadn't done it because we hadn't told them about it. So then we got dragged into a whole new argument, and that was just as bad; and sometimes if they said they didn't know, the other wouldn't believe them and would call them a liar; and we might hear that, when they were on the phone; and then we'd feel even worse the next time we saw them."

Erin is four years old, spunky, pert and verbal:

"My Daddy lives with a lady, not my Mommy. And when I stay at his place, my Mommy makes me always tell him to help me brush my teeth and give me a bath, because sometimes he doesn't. And my Mommy doesn't want the lady to help me, she always says to tell Daddy that; she says the lady isn't any good to help me, and my Daddy should do it. And he shouldn't go to work and let her put me to bed. So I tell him that. And sometimes he gets mad when I tell him."

Susan, at sixteen: " 'Get the money'—that's all Mom ever says when we're going to see Dad. That's about all she ever says to tell him.

"And sometimes, when we have a fight or if she's mad at me, she'll say, 'If you don't like it here you can tell your Dad you're going to go and live with him—see how he likes that.' But she knows I can't, even if I wanted to, even if he wanted me to, because he doesn't have a big enough place.

Dave is seven: "When I go to visit my Dad, my Mom always phones to talk to me; always when we are having supper. And then she'll tell me to tell my Dad to be sure I drink lots of milk and not pop and junk. And that makes him mad, every time I see him."

Hank is seven, too: "My Dad has sort of changed. He doesn't talk about my Mom much now. He just says not to tell her things he tells me. He says, 'Don't tell Mommy my business, and don't tell me hers.' So we aren't s'posed to tell her, when she asks. But my Mom tells us to tell him things. If I need some new jeans, for school, she says, 'Tell your Dad. Tell him you haven't got any jeans to wear, to go to school.' And once she made me go to visit him with an old pair, with a hole, and he bought me some new ones."

Sometimes the medium is the message, indeed.

And occasionally, of course, the message is more plaintive than cruel. Rita is four:

"Do you know what my Mommy tells me to tell my Daddy, when we see him? She always tells me to tell him, 'Do you want to come back?' I always tell him. And he always says, 'No.' And I tell my Mommy that. He won't come back. He gots a moustache, now."

9
Lovers and Step-parents

I've mentioned before that divorced kids are greatly protective of both their parents. With the obvious exceptions of children who have been deeply hurt or embittered, these youngsters are profoundly interested in the happiness of their parents, and much concerned that parents whom they see as having been cheated by life have an opportunity for happiness in the future. One child especially concerned is Lance, twelve; he is slight, fair-haired, speaks with a slight lisp, and is heavily freckled, sun-burned.

"Sometimes, my Mom sees a fortune-teller or somebody like that. She does it pretty often. And they'll tell her 'You'll meet this new man,' or something like that. And then she comes home and tells me. Or she'll read her horoscope in the newspaper, and it'll say, 'There's a new romance coming.'

"I always tell her it's probably true. She'll meet somebody she really likes, who likes her. I dunno whether I'd like that, but she would. I guess it all depends on what kind of guy she meets. But she wants to; so I guess I hope she does. Someday. Maybe when I'm older."

When a new or potentially new parent actually comes along the children respond strongly, if silently.

Intense and critical interest is focussed on new romantic interests in parental lives—though I was surprised by one discovery. In some areas touching their lives after a divorce children are very reflective, almost, on occasion, superstitious; but in matters touching on the love-lives of their now-separated parents, most responses reflect pure pragmatism.

Janet is five. Of the two years since her parents' separation she spent most of the first year with her father, his lover and her two daughters—but has spent the past year with her mother:

"Daddy only has Fran, now. She's my friend—my other big sister. I miss her a lot. She's my Daddy's friend, too, but more sort of like his wife.

"I had to sleep with Daddy and Fran on my own special little bed in their room. I didn't like that 'cause they were always making so much noise in their bed; jumping around and stuff; and they keeped me awake all the time. At night and in the morning, too. 'Cause they made a lots of noise and they wouldn't let me get to sleep. And they would keep me awake all night."

Shelley is nine: "Mom has lots of boy-friends but I don't like them anyhow 'cause they're mean to me. Mom would promise me that we'd go to my aunt's; and then a boy-friend would come, and he'd say, 'Do you want to go out for dancing?' and they'd go, and then I couldn't go out to my aunt's.

"I'd like a boy-friend for my Mom if he was nice, and if he was nice to kids—and if he had kids 'cause then I'd have someone to play with. Mom says that if she doesn't get married again and if she doesn't have any more kids that she might adopt one or two. That might be OK. But when my mother goes out with men they're always too young. And then she'll say, 'I'll have to drop it 'cause he's too young.'"

May is nine: "I dunno about Mom's boy-friend; I don't like him very much, he doesn't pay attention to me. Anyway, he's always asleep when he's here."

And Angie is four; her parents separated last year:

"My Mommy gets Michael to fix stuff for us. Michael's one of her boy-friends. She gots lots of boy-friends. Michael gived her our new record player. He's fat. I don't like him. I don't like her boy-friends; they take our toys away, always are putting our toys away somewhere.

"I don't like them and I can't tell you why; it's a bad word. Well—I'll tell you; but it's a bad word; I have to say a bad word. OK, then. I hate Mommy's boy-friends 'cause when they stay at our house they make lovies all the time with my Mommy; that's the bad word.

"And then, every time I come in, when I want to sleep with my Mommy, all the time they are making lovies. So I look in my Mommy's room, and I see them making lovies and I can't sleep with my Mommy. And I go back to my room, and I cry. So I hate them. 'Cause she just wants to make lovies and not sleep with me. Maybe I'll run away. Someday."

Step-parents and new lovers can be an unexpected success, can even help to heal the scars from a divorce. But I found resentment and rejection very common—and thereby hang some important cautionary tales.

It's worth noting that, for many if not most children, there's little differentiation made between step-parents and lovers. Younger children, especially solitary children, may see step-parents as a means of procuring company in the form of new brothers or sisters. Older children, those over ten or twelve, seem to differentiate little between boy-friends or girl-friends and step-parents. The two exceptions to this blurring come, first, when a step-parent is seen as an instrusive factor in the home; and second, when a parent is perceived to have wronged the family by "running-off" to marry someone else. In one of the most dramatic examples of this latter situation, I was given the following story by a twenty-five-year-old named Gary:

"My mother re-married and I get along OK with her new husband; I was eighteen when she married again and I was away at college so I don't see him much and when I do we get along fine; and she seems happier, so that's fine.

"But I have a friend, George, whose mother left his father, just about the way mine did. And his mother moved from Scotland, where they lived, and lived with this guy in the States for a few years, until her divorce came through, and then married him. That was about thirteen years ago, when George was eleven, and for years he never spoke to her or wrote to her or even acknowledged that she was legally married. He calls her 'that whore,' and he never even admits that she has a regular home, and a family. She and her new husband had a couple of kids.

"George and his brother mostly lived in boarding schools until they were grown up; didn't see much of their father, either. George's mother would write to him and send him presents for his birthday or whatever; and he'd send them back without opening them. Then once, when he was about fifteen, he wrote to her and said something like, 'Never mention that man' and 'I do not think of you as my mother,' or words to that effect.

"So then he started keeping the mail—and he would send her a Christmas card every year; he still does, but always just a printed card, with his name written on it, never 'love', or anything, and always addressed to her former name—his father's name—not her new married name.

"George lives in Chicago now and she lives in Detroit so they are pretty close, but when she writes and asks him to visit, says she'll send a plane ticket, he just ignores it.

"And she is so intimidated, I guess, by him, that when she writes him, almost every week, she just signs her letters, 'Your friend,' because she knows he still won't accept her."

Intense and critical interest can lead to extraordinary behaviour patterns in children.

Gillian was ten when her parents moved apart—twelve when her mother re-married.

"We lived south of London and my brother and I were away at school most of the year; he was two years younger. The thing is that we both decided we hated Mummy and the man she married although they were both always very kind to us; and even now, at twenty-seven, I don't think I've forgiven her—but I'm not sure for what.

"We made a pact, my brother and I, that we would watch them and spy on them and keep records, and report only to each other. And we swore solemnly never to tell anyone else.

"So when we were home for holidays or weekends, which was quite often, we'd wait until they thought we were both asleep. Then we would creep part way down the stairs, to a landing where it was dark. And we would crouch there, in the dark, and watch them in the sitting room, for hours.

"We would make notes about things they said, write them all down; then, later, we would read over the notes and talk about them and search for mysterious, terrible meanings in the things they said.

"What was monstrous, I suppose, was that we never gave them any hint of how we felt or what we were doing. We were always very polite with them; I would give Mummy a hug when I went up to bed; then, in half-an-hour, I'd be back, hiding on the stairs.

"When only one of us was home, as often happened, we would do the same thing, and keep a sort of diary for the other. Sometimes we'd save them, until we were together, and sometimes we'd write to each other at school, where there was no chance of our mother or her husband finding them.

"When I was at school I kept the diaries under my mattress and when I was at home I hid them behind a loose board in my closet. If my mother found out, even now, I'm sure she'd be terribly shocked and hurt.

"But the thing was, we never saw our father—and I guess we blamed Mummy for that, and her husband. It wasn't very rational I suppose, but it's how we felt.

"I still feel that way, I suppose. I'm not sure whether I still hate him—her husband—and her; but I suppose I must. And when I got married I made it very clear that I was not prepared to have children. I don't like them very much, actually, anyway—and I certainly would never subject any child to what we went through.

"I still see my Mummy—and we write to each other a lot. But I have never felt free with her or her husband. And when we visit England I never inflict them on my husband. I have to spend a day or two with them, for convention's sake, so I send my husband along to do something else."

Harry is twenty-four. Three years after his parents' separation his father re-married; two years after that, at fifteen, he went to live with his father because of disputes with his mother.

"Dad's second wife just had him by the nose, all the time;

anything she wanted was OK and everything she didn't like was strictly forbidden. I'd never seen him like that. He used to fight a lot with Mom; but with her it was, 'Yes, dear. No, dear. Anything you say, dear.' It was sickening.

"About the only time he stood up to her at all was over me, a few times. She thought I should have a newspaper delivery route, for God's sake; she said any boy who didn't deliver papers was just a lazy punk—that I should be earning money to buy my own clothes and stuff like that. She'd be all sweet to me to my face, cook me special dishes and all, and then bitch about me to him, behind my back; but quite often I'd hear her, she wasn't very smart about it.

"She seemed always to be jealous of the slightest thing we did together, the smallest amount of time we were together. If she decided she wanted to go to bed early, or she was doing something else, we might be talking or maybe playing a few games of chess in the living-room. And she'd come to the top of the stairs, about every ten minutes, and holler, 'When are you coming to bed? You're keeping me awake.' Well, how could we keep her awake playing chess, for God's sake?

"Or if Dad gave me a few dollars for spending money, or for a date, he'd have to sneak it to me. Because she was always bitching that he gave me too much. I think that was just her way of saying she wanted more for herself—and God knows she made sure she never went short.

"Even now, at Christmas she does a turkey and a whole Christmas dinner and makes a big deal, but it all feels phoney; he still can't get away from her long enough to have a decent visit with any of us.

"It's like she has him hypnotized. I s'pose it's sex, partly; and partly, I think, he's terrified that he'll screw up again, that he'll have two marriages blow up in his face. The thing I find it a bit hard to forgive him for, I think we all do, is that he's a bright guy; I think he knows what she's doing, how she has made a gap between him and us—and he goes along with it. That's hard to forgive—but I guess it hurts him, too; it's the price he seems prepared to pay, though; and we have to pay, too."

Even the "best" step-parental relationships can rub enough to raise social blisters. Betty is sixteen. A few months ago her mother re-married.

"They just went away, quietly, for the weekend, and got married. We knew they were going to about two months before—they had been going together for over a year. He told the three of us kids and asked us how we felt, at summer one night. We said OK. What could we say?

"There are just two things, though: for one, they both work, pretty hard, I guess, so they aren't home very much. And when they are they like to spend a lot of their time together, alone. So Mom doesn't have much time for us now—as much time. Still, it's better than before they were married; at least she's here now. Then she was always sleeping over at his apartment, or coming home about three o'clock in the morning.

"The other thing is that he really tries to protect her a lot, I think. So if I'm having a fight with her maybe he'll interfere and take her side, of course, all the time. So how can I talk to her or fight things out with her? 'Cause he's just always there; all the time.

"He's really good to her, you know; that's good—I like to see her getting spoiled a bit, getting flowers and stuff. But sometimes I wish he just wasn't around, every single time I'd like to talk to my Mom; 'cause a lot of the time I feel he really doesn't approve of me—or like my friends. As long as she doesn't complain, why should he? He tries to be a sort of disciplinarian; I wish he'd just quit it."

This accusation of "bossiness" was a constant refrain—and was applied as much to lovers as to step-parents.

Linda and her sister, Mary, are fourteen and twelve:

Linda: "My Mom has a boy-friend; she likes him, and enjoys his company. But he tells her things like he doesn't think my girl-friend should sleep over on week nights and he doesn't like it when we have pop and chips every night. And I say it's none of his business."

Mary: "I don't like Mom's boy-friend that much. Because he's too picky. Like, he sees something in our room and it isn't clean and he says it looks like a pigpen. Everything has to be clean for him. That's his way. I don't like him. I don't think everything has to be perfect; I don't think it's any of his business. He's not my father.

"He doesn't really pick on me. He doesn't say anything like that to me, but he'll ask—he'll tell my Mom, right? And she'll tell us. I told her it was none of his business and she said she knew.

"I guess it's hard for her. I guess I just don't think anyone would fit my Mom. Only my Dad would. Because he's my only Dad—my real Dad."

If not "bossiness", then sometimes "pushiness."

Anna is eleven: "When we go over to see my father and his girl-friend, I never tell anyone; I don't want my friends to know that my parents are separated.

"His girl-friend is OK; she's quite pretty. But when we go over there she always forces us to put pony tails in our hair. I don't really feel comfortable around her. Sometimes when we're there she makes us call her 'Mom'. And I already call my own mother 'Mom' so I don't want to. We stayed over about twice, but mostly it's just for the day. I don't like to stay over, with her."

A variation, involving a step-parent, comes from a lady in her early forties, whose parents divorced when she was about thirty, and whose father re-married five years later:

"I just don't like her; she's pushy. She is forever writing to all the children, all four of us, inviting us for a family reunion or suggesting we should all bring our families and spend Christmas with them. Well, really. I scarcely know the woman; I gather she's taking good care of Dad, he's got a bit of a heart condition now. That's fine. But no one is taking care of mother and we all have our own families to worry about. I guess if we'd known her when we were small it would be different, but after forty is a bit late to start in on a new mother."

But the verdict isn't always adverse. Here, as just one example, is Andrew, fourteen, who is comfortable with the former secretary who now shares his father's home and life:

"Yeah, she's nice; she's a good cook. When we go over there, every other weekend, it's just like our home, you know; we have our own room and everything, just waiting for us. I guess she's a good wife for him." His brother Lance agrees: "She's really nice, his new wife. I like her."

There are two essential points made by all these children in their observations of new friends, lovers, spouses found by either parent.

First, the kids want honesty. They want to be allowed to share in the indices of any new happiness, and to do so without the need to compare "now" with "then", the cheap, overt comparisons of this new lover with that discarded marital partner. Also the kids need direct responses to direct questions. It's silly to say, as I have, "Never mind. It's nothing that should interest you," when an eight-year-old asks, "How come you buy stuff for your girl-friend and you never give Mommy any presents any more?" I don't think I've ever adequately coped with that sort of question, spoken or silent, but I'm learning. For openers, truth is usually the best bet. It's acceptable to tell your child you no longer bake a cake for Daddy's birthday, or buy a gift for Mommy, because that's something done only by people who are living together. OK, too, to say one is buying a flower or gift for "someone else", because of affection.

Children are only amused by attempts to play down or mask a relationship with a new man or woman; those shabby, small deceptions only fill them with embarrassment. They don't resent new happiness, they celebrate it—unless it's the selfish and immature sort of joy that shuts them out. And if your child wonders why you no longer buy or make gifts or surprises for the other parent, it's easy to suggest *they* might wish to do so—and to help them. It's bitterness that children find confusing and hurtful. Magnanimity is the best nourishment for their love and their confidence in themselves and their parents; it's the least expensive and most precious of all gifts.

Second, the kids are interested in substantive developments in their parents' lives, but they don't want to play analyst or unwilling witness to self-destructive behaviour by a parent. Many survivors of the marital crash begin working out their new destiny through a series of not-very-serious relationships. That may be fine for them, but it's only a source of total confusion for their children. Divorced kids can cope very well with new friends and casual relationships developed by their parents; cope very well, and joyfully, too, with serious new relationships. But if you are celebrating your freedom by playing musical beds save those activities for your private moments away from the children; don't inflict your lovers on your kids until you are ready to take them seriously yourself.

10
Portraits

Before we move on to some final conclusions, I'd like you to meet
four particular divorced kids. Up till now I've split individual
interviews between different chapters so it's been difficult to get a
sense of the uniqueness of each of the children. Now that the
groundwork has been laid there's time to meet a few divorced kids
in greater depth. Not surprisingly, Chris, John, Jan and Gail refer
back to topics we've already touched. All of them however, are also
looking forward.

Chris is fourteen and has been separated from her father for about
eighteen months; she, her mother and two younger brothers
moved to her maternal grandmother's home.

Chris has short, brown hair topping an average height and
build. The hair, done in bangs, sweeps away from her side parting,
curving down to the full fall of hair at the nape of her neck. Her
manner is tidy, contained, controlled; her expressions, however,
are over-sophisticated for her age, brittle, a trifle bellicose. Sometimes, after a considerable pause, her answers would arrive in a
rush of words, her tone and facial expression challenging, as if to
say, "Okay, you asked for it; see how you like this."

"My parents were fighting a lot, that's why they got separated.
I think she needed to find out what she wanted and he needed to
find out what he wanted. Like, it was my Mom's fault, too. She'd
always be yelling all the time, and she'd get mad at him for the
slightest thing. Like, if he came in late from work, she'd scream and
yell, start screaming at him that he was 'never in the house,' and
stuff like that. And then the fighting would start. I'd get sent to my
room or I'd go and watch TV while they were fighting—but I could

still hear them.

"But my Dad has a pretty good temper, too, once he gets mad. Like, about three years ago, there was a party at our house, and everybody was drinking a little bit, and he and my Mom got to fighting and yelling. And he started chasing her all around the house; and then she runs outside, starts running down the road, and he gets the car, just starts up and takes off, and tries to run her down. He didn't get her, though; she jumped in the ditch.

"My Mom and Dad got married really young; he went straight from his Mom and got married, so he never had a chance to find out what he really wanted. That's why I don't think he'll ever come back; he wants a chance to find out what he really wants, without a bunch of kids around to look after.

"And my Mom, she just had to get married. See, she was pregnant, with me, and she was only sixteen, so she had to get married. That's what she told me. Like, she had me when she was sixteen, right after they got married.

"And she always tells me that she could have gone on to college, could have done anything. But she had me and so then she just had to get married; and then she had my brothers.

"And she'll go on at me, a lot. She'll say, 'You know it's just not my fault, mine and Jason's.' (He's my Dad.) She'll say, 'You weren't getting along with Jason, you know, you fought with him all the time, so we just had to separate; so you can't just blame me and Jason; it was your fault, too.'

"And then she'll say, like, if she didn't have me so early, when she was so young, then she would have been able to get along with Jason, she wouldn't have been fighting with him all the time, so much."

(Chris plucked continuously at some bits of invisible lint on her skirt during this portion of the conversation; the hard edge stayed in her voice, her manner was still truculent—but her eyes were down, her hands constantly picking, picking at her skirt.)

"I dunno. Maybe she's right. I still don't get along with him, you know. I don't phone him. I haven't seen him for about five months. The last time I saw him, we had this big row. Like, I was sitting in his place, and I just asked him if it was my fault and some other stuff he didn't like—and he just slaps me. He calls me 'Motor mouth,' and then he just slaps me, right across the face. So I guess she's right—he doesn't like me very much. He was always yelling at me, before, and he still does. Like, he always wants kids to be perfect or something. I don't think he likes kids very much, really. You know, kids aren't born to touch things, or to do things, they might only break stuff or get into trouble. So it's not very comfortable, being around him.

"But if it's my fault, it's their fault, too. She didn't have to get pregnant, with me; they didn't have to have me. She didn't have to fool around, with him, when she was fifteen, sixteen. So they can't blame it all on me."

Chris's former home, outside Cleveland, was very comfortable and spacious, and it was there she developed her love of horses. Now, living with her mother, two brothers and a grandmother, her physical life is crowded, rarely private, in the heart of the city rather than in a tree-filled country atmosphere. Her grandparent's home is a modest bungalow; it is small and made to seem smaller by a clutter of heavy, dark furniture. Three people would fill its single floor; seven now live in it.

"I don't get as much things as I used to. We weren't rich or anything, but we weren't poor. We were a little over medium—we had a nice house, and a barn, and a swimming pool, and horses. He still lives there, my Dad. See, my Mom and him had a huge fight, and she just started packing and brought me and my brothers down here. That's why he got to keep the house.

"And now, my Mom is always worried about money. She says we have to stay here, with her parents, for another two years, until she saves up enough money to buy a house. But she's crazy; she's worried about money and she sends me to this dumb school which costs over $6,000 a year; and I don't need it, I just want to go to horse college, learn to work with horses. And I'm too dumb for school, anyway; when you're in Grade Eight and you are using a Grade Four spelling book—that's dumb. So I don't see where school is necessary.

"Now that she works—she started just before the separation—she just ignores us kids. But that's OK. I don't care. This is sure better than living with the two of them together.

"But it's sure crowded. I used to have my own room, with a big double bed, but it's really crowded here. Now, I have to sleep with my Mom and she's moving around, all over the bed, all night, so I can't sleep.

"My Dad still gets me stuff. He bought me a ten-speed bike, and a little mini-bike, with a motor. And he buys things for the boys, too, a lot. Because they know they can get away with it, with him. My Mom would say, 'No.' But with him, they keep asking him and he always says, 'Okay. I'll buy you that. Now just be quiet.' So they always get it. And they know that."

"Charlie is my mother's boy-friend; he's here all the time or else she's talking to him on the phone every chance she gets. I don't mind.

"Charlie is short and bald; and he's old-fashioned. He's always saying children don't do this or don't do that. And he's old; he's forty-five and she's thirty-two. I don't like him. He's always saying how his kid is really under his control; his kid does as he's told, he says, and if he had me, I'd be doing what he wanted, too. He's so bossy, and I'm not his kid.

"I think she's pretty serious about him; I think she'd like to marry him. He's supposed to be separated, but his wife still lives in his house. Mom really gets upset; like, she cried when she found out that Dad had a girl-friend, but she had a boy-friend already. And she cried when Charlie dropped her for a while—that happens quite a bit. And then she cries when they start up together again.

"I think she's using Charlie a bit, too—to make my Dad jealous—only he isn't. I don't think my Mom wants my Dad back or anything like that. I think she just wants to provoke him. Anyway, he has his own girl-friend. I don't know whether she lives with him, in the house, or not. Anyway, I don't care what she does with Charlie. I can just go out with my own friends, and go riding whenever I can."

(Gavin, Chris's younger brother, is nine years old. His attention span was so short as to be virtually undetectable; he was totally unresponsive, wandering off onto any topic that took his fancy, regardless of the questions. Only once, when asked if his mother was likely to marry Charlie, did he snap to anxious, angry attention: "No way! She's going to marry my Dad! She's never going to marry anybody else! And she hasn't got a boy-friend, anyway! Charlie isn't her boy-friend. She hardly ever sees Charlie, I don't even know who Charlie is.")

When it comes to looking for guides to her own future life, Chris blames all her parents' problems on sex, and wants none of it:

"One thing, though, the way they all behave, I don't ever want to get married. Never. Well, I guess I might if he was a very rich man, otherwise, no. And I don't want to have any children. I guess if I got married I might have to adopt. But I don't want to do *that*, to get pregnant; not ever."

John, nearly fifteen, has stunning verbal skills. He is a "golden boy," compact, well-muscled, sandy-haired, tanned. His hair is close-cropped, his eyes hazel, wide-set, direct. His poise and his unhesitating speech are a bit disconcerting, the words laid out, neatly, like even rows of brick, with no fumbling or waiting for the best phrase; each thought tidily mortared, the well-rounded sentences tapped fondly into place with the verbal trowel. He sat on his bed as we talked. The only sign of agitation through an hour's taping was his almost constant physical movement: rolling onto his back; sitting, for a moment, tailor fashion; stretching his arms, testing one muscle against another; crossing and uncrossing his legs; rolling onto his stomach to prop his face in his hands; then arching up to sit on his heels; every movement smooth, supple; every joint and tendon oiled and silent; in brief still periods he would pull sternly at a short lock of frontal hair.

"We used to hear them quarrelling a lot for about three months before they separated. Like, at that time they knew that my younger sister and I knew they were going to get separated and they didn't try to conceal the fact from us. They never told us what they were quarrelling about and I never really asked because I didn't care. But my sister was really affected a lot. Every single night when it was time to go to bed she'd cry until she went to sleep. I guess, being eight years old at that time (three years ago) it was a real blow to her. She was really close to my Dad.

"Every Friday Dad used to pick me up after school. That was when I asked him if they were going to get a divorce. So every Friday after that, when he picked me up, we would talk about it.

He told me some things, he sort of won me over to his side. He told me some things that weren't true, about my mother. He told me a lot of things that were true, too, but he made me feel sort of negatively toward my mother. For example he told me that Mom was constantly lying to him, and insulting his relatives. That wasn't true.

"Anyway, then I heard my Mom talking on the telephone to a friend, and I found out that she was ready to leave. So I told my Dad, that Friday. I think I even surprised him. He knew that it was going to happen but he didn't know that Mom's mind was made up yet. He was surprised. Then they separated, that week.

"I was upset. I knew it was for the best because it was better than them constantly quarrelling. But I was upset. I wished they could have stayed together because it was more fun that way, and we could have kept our old house and our dog and everything.

"But I'm sure it was for the best because someone would have ended-up getting hurt. And I sure didn't want that." (A real, but rarely-expressed fear of physical violence is a common theme among children of between seven and fifteen. They can't comprehend how adults can argue with such brutality and rage without resorting to blows.)

"Anyway, I mostly understood it was better. But not for my sister. Not then. It was really very hard for her. After all, all her friends grew up with a Mom and a Dad and I guess at eight years old, without a Mom and a Dad, gee, where are you?

"I don't really mind that my parents got separated but one thing still makes me mad: I wish, I just wish that they had waited about two years—just waited until my sister was old enough to understand what was happening. She was only eight and it was just impossible for her. They should have waited until it was safe for her, but I don't think parents consider their kids much when they separate. They just should really consider the children, and if the children are too young, they just shouldn't do it for a while. My parents didn't think about my sister.

"My sister was a lot closer to my Dad than my Mom. I was a lot closer to my Mom than my Dad. And on the outside she seemed OK—kind of enthusiastic about moving into the new apartment and everything . . . But she was always crying. It's going to affect her for the rest of her life, I think.

"I can remember at night, lying in my room here in the apartment, just lying there, and all of a sudden there would be the sound of this sobbing, and I used to feel so sorry for her. 'Oh, God,' I thought. 'There's this little kid, eight years old, who cries every night.' She'd have bad dreams and wake up in the middle of the night yelling, 'Daddy! Daddy!' I couldn't stand it. It was really terrible. I'm adjusted to it now but I know my little sister is still worrying about it, thinking maybe it was her fault for some reason. I don't talk to her about it. It upsets her, so I don't raise it.

"I don't think she'll ever be really secure, stop wondering why it happened, if she could have stopped it. I mean, I guess every kid wonders if it could have been their fault, somehow; I know I did. I certainly considered it, at least for a second, when it first happened, when I first found out. But I thought 'No, it couldn't be me. I've never done anything that bad.' But I wanted to be sure, and I talked to my Mom and my Dad and asked them, and they made it perfectly clear, even in the back of my subconscious that it wasn't my fault. And there was nothing I could do about it—the only way it could be solved was if they wanted it to be solved, and they didn't.

"But this terrible night, about three days after they separated, I was in bed, lying in bed thinking about it. And then there was this screaming, and my little sister ran out of her room yelling, 'It's all my fault. It's all my fault.' She was pretty young, of course, so she might think that, so it was really hard for her. But I don't think that she thinks that now."

At eleven, Jan seems unsure of herself, introspective, nervous. She is fair, slim, pretty with large brown eyes that welled tears, silently, several times as we spoke; she would wipe them off her cheeks absently, with the back of her hand. When I asked if she was too distressed to go on talking, she said, "No. It's OK. I just can't make them stop."

"It wasn't nobody's fault," she says, "nobody's at all, because they just didn't like each other any more. I guess sometimes I feel like maybe it was my fault, but not very often. Sometimes, though—a little bit."

(She blinked rapidly, sniffled a little, wiped her nose on the sleeve of her nightdress, then thought better of that, found a facial tissue, blew impressively into it, and continued): "Well, maybe sometimes parents just love their kids too much; and so they don't want us to see them fighting, or hear them fighting, and so they probably got separated because of that. That's what I thought, sometimes. I don't know."

John and Jan have had three years to grow accustomed to life without their father:

John: "I guess it's made me a little more independent, because now I don't have a father living with me. I sort of have to make up for that, now, don't I? I think my Mom maybe has more trust in me now, gives me more responsibility, trusts me more.

"I have to try extra hard, now, to be close to my Mom, to get closer to her; and the extra closeness with my Mom, well—it kind of makes up for not having much time with my Dad, not being very close with him, I guess.

"I still remember when I was young, and my Mom and Dad were both there; it was a much more secure feeling. But it doesn't really affect me; but when I was younger it really affected me there for quite a while. Quite a bit. It was really queer, to have only one parent I could go crying to. Like, if I had a problem I couldn't go to my Mom about—didn't want to go to my Mom about—then I'd have to wait for the next Saturday, when I saw my Dad. And by then it was too late. I couldn't wait.

"But I've learned to wait. It's a lot easier now. I save them up, till Saturdays.

"I really think that this way my Dad and I have gotten closer, gotten a better relationship. Because now, when we are together, we make more of an effort of it. Like, in the summer, some of my friends hardly ever see their Dads, maybe only once a month or so; but I see my father every week. Now I feel pretty lucky, compared to some of my friends—but in the beginning I used to wish I could see him a lot more.

"My Dad often says that someday I'll go and live with him. I used to think that would be great. The first few months after my parents got divorced, I used to say that as soon as I was old enough I would go and live with my Dad.

"But now I'm not so sure. I think I kind of like it the way it is, right now. You know, my Dad has some funny ways. And I don't like some of the ways he thinks that children should grow up, be brought up.

"He really doesn't have much trust in us at all. He's a little over-protective, I think, and I don't like that very much because, when I'm with him, or when he is looking after me, it really limits me. For example, he doesn't like me going on bike trips with my friends and things like that. He really doesn't trust me to be responsible, so that just makes it harder to grow up, doesn't it?

"The other thing I don't like was the lies he told me about our mother. He told me that my mother drank too much and sometimes got drunk. I'd been brought up with the idea that people shouldn't drink or smoke or anything. And I started to get so I didn't feel too good about her. Then, after we'd been living alone with Mom for about a few months, she told me those things weren't true. I don't know why I believed her; I guess I never saw her drunk, and I just trusted her enough to believe her.

"I didn't really get mad at my Dad for telling me those things; I don't hate him for it. That's probably what I would have done, too, if I'd been him. Because he just wanted my sister and me to be on his side; because he loved my sister and I, and I guess he loved us just as much as my Mom. So he wanted me on his side. But I wish he hadn't said those things, just the same.

"Mom is a lot freer, now, not as strict or as mean. It's like she's forgotten things like you mustn't ever drink or smoke or swear. She says now, if you want to swear, or drink, or smoke, then go ahead; but it won't make you a better person.

"I'm always with my Mom, now—I only see my Dad once a week; I didn't use to feel very comfortable, talking to her about some stuff. But now that she's freer, if I have a problem I can talk to my Mom. Before, when they were fighting and everything, I never used to feel I had anyone to talk to. So I'm pretty glad I live with my Mom. I really get along a bit better with her, can talk with her a bit better, about problems."

(John hesitates for a moment, bites his lower lip thoughtfully, hugs his knees, flexes the fingers of one hand and looks at them, almost as though for the first time. His speech slows a bit now). "I wouldn't want my Mom to get married, again. Well—I wouldn't object, that wouldn't be my place. But—well, I don't think that she's the type that would do good in a marriage. I mean, when they were having trouble, they could have gone to a marriage counsellor, but my Mom didn't want any of that; she just wanted the freedom of not being married. I think maybe that's why it didn't work in the first place, because she just wanted to be free; and that's pretty hard, when you are married.

"I guess at one time, she must have loved my father, or she wouldn't have got married to him; so it must be saddening for her, that it didn't work. But I don't think she'd want to take the chance of all that happening again. I don't think it would be a good idea."

Despite this, Jan, thinks her brother would really like her mother to re-marry:

"See, I think he really misses our Dad. Pretty often he says, 'I wish we had a bigger man around the house.'

"I think that's 'cause he's the only boy. So he feels left out a lot, when my Mom and I do stuff together. If my Mom got married again, then he'd have someone else, another boy—a man for him to do stuff with."

"I really didn't used to like my Dad, all that much. I mean after he and my Mom separated. I didn't think much of him and I couldn't get to know him all that much, and I didn't care.

"But then I stayed with him for a whole weekend; just me and his girl-friend and then I got to like him a lot more. My brother wasn't with me, that weekend, so I got to know him a lot more. It was much better than the Saturdays, because I saw him for four days in a row, just by myself. And now I like him quite a bit."

Even so, Jan has problems common to many divorced kids in resolving the discrepancies between what her father tells her and what she sees in her daily life:

"My Mom doesn't have so much money now. Not any more. Before, when we all lived together, he would give her money to do the shopping. Now she has to support herself. But my Dad gives her money every month. I wasn't supposed to know how much it was, but I saw the cheque, so I know.

"And my Dad says the money is to buy groceries. But he says

she always uses it for cigarettes and junk for herself. But I don't think she does. I think she just uses it for stuff for us.

"My Mom gets pretty mad when my Dad talks to me instead of when he's supposed to talk to her. Sometimes she gets so mad that she cries. Like, he is supposed to tell her, for two weeks ahead of time, that he wants to have us for a weekend. That's the rule. From the court. But pretty often he doesn't tell her that soon. He'll phone me when she's at work, and tell me to come the next day, and I should tell my mother. And that really makes her mad. And then, sometimes, she says things about him—I won't tell you what—and says I should tell him. But I don't.

"He doesn't say mean things about her, like to me. Just, sometimes, when he's talking to her on the phone, like about when I'm going to be home, he just makes a funny face when he hangs up the phone.

"My Mom seems quite a bit happier, now. She has this job, and she gets her hair done more; it's a little different colour. She wears tighter clothes, now. And she goes out a lot more; sometimes her friends come here. She seems younger. I guess she's maybe more fun now. Not at first. But now.

"Mom has boy-friends. I like all of them, 'cept one. Sometimes I heard her; she gets upset and asks him to leave, and he just stays and stays. And he kind of tries to impress us and brings us this candy and stuff; and we tell him that he shouldn't do that because it's bad for our teeth; his teeth are awful and he's eating this candy all the time. It's how you feel; I don't want to have a friend just because I eat their candy. But I like my Dad's girl-friend. She's nice, and she likes me."

How do they feel about marriage? Jan says, "When I get older I'll get married and all that—have kids; I hope I will. Lots of people stay married—for a long time anyway. My Mom and Dad were married for quite a long time. I hope, I just hope, that I don't ever get separated, if I can get married, someday. I don't think I would; I really wouldn't want to—get separated. But mostly I don't think that's going to happen. Not if I get married to someone I like. 'Cause, see, my Mom and Dad don't like each other. But I wouldn't get married with somebody I didn't like."

John has thought about marriage, too, and articulates his

views with great care and precision:

"I think I have a much higher sense of an ideal. See, I think it's possible to have a good marriage if you really know what you want before you start. I probably wouldn't just settle for anything, I have a real ideal in mind.

"A lot of my friends, my older friends, get married, and I wonder. I think there are more sort of convenience marriages, and things are looser—much looser than I want. That probably doesn't work too well.

"So I don't feel totally against it. But I don't feel in a rush for it, either. And I think, after being through what I've been through, I'd have to be a lot more careful before taking the plunge. I have friends who have been through broken homes and they are just totally against it altogether; a lot of them just don't ever see it happening for them. I don't feel that strongly about it—not quite that strongly. But I'd wait for my ideal."

Lastly, Gail. At eighteen Gail is very poised outwardly, with a smoothly-tanned complexion, burnished hair, a level gaze from green eyes; her manner, when her mother was present, was shy, withdrawn, almost totally self-effacing; immediately her mother left the room she became more animated, more assured—even her posture straightened, her gestures became more assertive. Her brother, two years older, has lived with her father since her parents' separation.

"It was about five years ago when they separated; but I think it had started a few years before that. They really used to have some terrific fights about my brother, and generally my Dad would support him and my Mom would be really mad at him.

"It all started when he was growing up, getting into his teens, and he started to get into a little bit of trouble, which, of course, he'd bring home. They'd argue about it and my Mom would start in on my Dad, and tell him he was just incapable of handling my brother.

"So it all evolved into a problem between my parents, and how they would handle my brother. They just couldn't agree. Quite a few of those arguments happened in front of me—they didn't seem to care about that.

"Then, one day, I was in the recreation room, and I saw my father going out to the garage with two suitcases. And my brother was upstairs, and he went, too. And my father didn't talk to me, didn't say anything at all, and neither did my mother. And my brother just got in the car, with my father. It was weird, as if no one in the house wanted to admit what was going on, what was happening, right then. It was like they didn't believe it was happening at all, like it was just a bad dream.

"So then, I got the same; I didn't want to talk about it at all either. I didn't want to talk about it, or admit it to my friends or anything. My brother always wanted to talk to me about it when I saw him, to see if I thought it was really his fault, or if Mom did — he had trouble talking to her — but I never wanted to discuss it with him. I suppose, in a way, I kind of blamed him almost as much as he blamed himself."

"You can't help feeling some sense of guilt. I think every child does. But maybe it would be worse if some parents stayed together and said, 'Look, we stayed together because of you kids, even though we wanted to separate and have our own lives.' Then the kids might feel even guiltier. And anyway, it can't all be the fault of just one person, can it? When you look at the responsibility for a marriage break-down, it just had to be all of us. It's selfish of me to say it wasn't even a little bit my fault—but I don't know how, or where, because I was so young, I didn't know what else to do.

"I miss my brother very much; when he first went to live with my father it was a long time, about eight months before I saw him again. We used to argue all the time and talk all the time, when he lived with us; even argue a lot about what channel to watch on TV. But it was weird with him gone, with having no one at all to talk to but one parent."

"When they separated and my brother decided to go live with my Dad I think maybe she was afraid I would too, if I had a choice, and then she wouldn't have as much money from him. I would like to have been given that choice, but I probably would have stayed with my Mother, anyway; I was a little closer to her, at that age, and I probably needed a woman for that transition into the teens, from twelve to thirteen, fourteen.

"But she was even hesitant about me seeing my brother. I guess she figured if I kept seeing my brother eventually I'd find a way to see my Dad. And we did sort of communicate, my Dad and I, through my brother. When I got a birthday present from my brother, for those two years, I knew it was from my father too. He'd just sort of smile at me, or wink, when he gave it to me. But I wouldn't tell my mother.

"I don't know exactly why he didn't just go to court and get permission to see me; I think maybe he wanted to keep things as cool as possible. He didn't want to make waves, and he knew that eventually she would cool off, let her fences down and let him see me. But for those first two years, I never saw him or talked to him.

"I remember once, when I guess I was fourteen, or maybe fifteen, I went to the telephone directory, to see if my Dad was listed in it. And my mother had ripped out that page; she was afraid I'd find his name and his number and maybe call him and talk with him. She was really bitter; you see, she used to tell him that if he didn't like it, the way things were, he could just get out. And then, when he did, she could hardly believe it, I suppose, and that's why she was so bitter.

"Quite often now I go down to my Dad's office, just drop in and visit with him. Sometimes I have lunch with my Dad, but I don't tell my Mom. It would only cause arguments. She knows I see him sometimes, when it's arranged, but I still don't think she likes it, even then.

"One problem was that after those two years I was really scared to be with him or see him. I mean, things change a lot in two years, and I wasn't sure what he'd be like. So anyway, when I see him now, just casually, or for lunch, I just keep it to myself. She'd just be asking all kinds of questions and saying really bitter things, and we'd have an argument and that would spoil it all, spoil having seen him, I mean. So I lie. I just say I had lunch at school, or with a girl-friend."

When we talked Gail had just had her eighteenth birthday that week:

"I know my mother was really bitter about the divorce. I've always known that, from the beginning. But I guess I've just realized that my father is bitter, too. He still has some real anger, I think. And it gets in the way; bitterness and anger always affect the children and hurt them.

"For my birthday, we were going out to dinner and I have really been looking forward to it. And then he said to me he didn't want my mother along. We've done it before, had dinner all together on my birthday: my Mom and Dad and my brother. So I didn't understand why he would say 'No' now. I guess that's when I realized there was still some bitterness on his side.

"He doesn't seem to understand that the greatest birthday, for me, would be to have our whole family, or what used to be our family, sit down to dinner together with no arguments, just pleasant conversation.

"So I phoned his office. I left a message with his secretary to say that mother was coming to dinner. I guess I was demanding it. I *was* demanding it. After all, it was *my* birthday. Then he called, later, to say that he was working late, he had a meeting, and he couldn't go to dinner, which I didn't know whether to believe or not.

"I didn't know my Dad could be almost childish enough to do that. Maybe he did work late. I don't know. Anyway, he said we'd all have dinner together on the weekend. But I haven't heard from him yet, and it's been four days. He's supposed to call me. I'm not going to call him. I can wait. I waited two years, once, didn't I, when Mom wouldn't let me see him? So I can wait, all right—for my eighteenth birthday dinner."

"My father really has wrong impressions of my mother, sometimes, but it's really her own fault. He keeps asking what she does with her days, how she keeps from just going crazy, sitting around all day. He says she should go out and work, develop some outside interest. It's nuts for her just to do nothing, he says.

"But the thing is, she *does* work; she got a job about a year ago. But she doesn't want him to know because she thinks the alimony payments would be cut off. She still has the same goal in life she's always had, even before the divorce—to have lots of money.

"But I think if he knew, he would think that much more of her. That really angers me. I've told her, and said I don't like it when I have to lie to him, but she won't even listen to me. She just wants to be sure she gets all the money she can.

133

"She's certainly a different kind of person now in terms of how she behaves. Before, she was definitely a housewife; you just had to look at her. But now, she works, she is going out, meeting the world.

"But she is still kind of cold, sort of brittle. One thing between my parents I really can't forgive them is that there was this lack, their failure to mention anything about love. I've never heard my mother, or my father, mention love, or say if they even loved each other, during the marriage. And that really hurts, more than everything.

"I really think my mother got married mainly because she wanted to get away from her home, get away from her mother. She was in her twenties then, but she really wasn't mature. I think she still isn't ready for marriage, and she's about forty-five. In some ways I think I'm more mature than she is.

"Sometimes, I think I'd like to get away from her and make my own life. But when I'm really down, when I just can't stand my mother any more, I go to see my uncle; he's about the only person I can really talk to—he's her older brother. And he really sets me straight and makes me feel better. He helps me to understand my mother better, too. I have to understand my mother, so that I can help her, so that eventually we'll really be able to talk. And so that I won't make the same mistakes as my mother.

"My uncle says, 'If you take this all too seriously, as you do now, you'll become bitter, too. And you'll become like your mother.' So I have to be very careful—to help her, and myself.

"The other thing that bothers me is that I don't think it's good that I have just the influence of my mother to guide me. She doesn't guide me too well, I don't think, because of the bitterness. So I have to be careful about that, too."

"I don't think my Mom will marry again. Well, she might, I suppose, if she met a really wealthy man; that's what she's really interested in—money. But she goes out a lot. She's a real swinger. I've met a lot of the guys she goes out with. A lot of them are real jerks. I certainly don't think they are using her; I think she's using them. She's definitely bitter towards men; that's why she likely won't marry. But I've met worse men than my father; she's gone out with some who are a lot worse.

"I don't know if my father will marry again. I won't be surprised if he does and I won't be surprised if he doesn't. I do think he's kind of having fun on his own.

"I think I would be jealous if he did marry again; it would kind of take something away from me. I met one of his girls; I wasn't jealous; but I sort of gave her the third degree. And she passed my test; she was OK. I sort of had to see if she was intelligent enough for my father, had to see she wasn't after just one thing—money. She wasn't phoney, though. One thing about my mother, she's really phoney. Anyway, if I approve of the woman my Dad likes, I don't think I'll mind if he marries.

"As for me, I have to keep comforting my mother by telling her I'll never get married—certainly not in the near future. She has a really bad attitude to marriage, because of her experience. So I always go along with her.

"I really think marriage should be thought about a lot. I think that maybe twenty-five, thirty years ago, people didn't think about marriage as seriously as they do now. They'd get married too quickly, after a three or four-month period. They didn't think what might happen in fifteen or twenty years and I think a lot of divorces today are from marriages like that. They didn't take the time to get to really know the person they thought they were going to live with for a whole lifetime; and I think you should. I don't know; someone I read said you never really know anybody until you sleep with them for a year and I don't think she was just being cynical.

"I don't think anyone should consider marriage under say, twenty-three or twenty-four. I don't have a serious boy-friend. I go out with two or three of them, not just any one. I don't care what anyone says, boys get serious a lot more quickly than girls, at least with me—I always find that and then I try to get out of it. I don't need that hassle, now. I don't need that serious commitment. I'd like to try and avoid it, do without it. As soon as I see it coming, I just get away from it. I've got too much more to do with life than be stuck down with some guy—one guy.

"I think I've been influenced on the positive side by what has happened to my parents; they've sort of given me a better outlook, even if they didn't intend to do that. Like when I was fifteen or sixteen, I was always scared—and only went out once or twice with the same fellow; I just didn't want to have to meet any demands made on me, if I kept going out with the same boy. Now if someone makes demands on me, I'm not scared at all. I'm a lot tougher now. I just don't meet those demands, just don't worry about them. So you get tougher, it's a positive thing, you see. I'm much more mature now because of it, I think, and now I can tell them where to go and where not to go, so it's not so bad now.

"The main thing is that what happened to my parents makes me much more cautious about entering into a relationship—any relationship—because I do not want all that to happen to me. My mother is really bitter. I don't want that for me."

"People should really think about separation too—think it through, before they do it. Mind you, I think a lot of people stay together because of the children, which is also the wrong reason, because years later they probably separate anyway, and then blame the children without realizing what they are doing to those kids."

PART FOUR
A Divorced Child's World

It's not possible to spend a few hundred hours discussing divorce with children who've experienced it without speculating about "patterns" and looking for "norms." There seemed to be several common to many of the children who agreed to talk about their feelings; but unlike the norms beloved by social psychologists, these were arrived at independently. Divorced kids don't often compare experiences with their friends; so any widely-held gut feelings are very strong evidence about the emotional impact of divorce.

First, the caveats: the generalities of response in this chapter are just that; they applied widely to the demographic slice interviewed for this book, but it was just a slice. Further, the views suggested here derive from the most common situations, in which the following usually apply:

The children live with their mother, but see their father frequently.

Whatever the emotional traumas of the marital separation, the children were not exposed to frequent violence or frequent drunkenness.

The parents believe the arrangements for the children to be rational, civilized, loving.

With those limits firmly in place, it's possible to generalize with considerable success about divorced kids and their feelings about:

1. MARRIAGE

Divorced kids certainly give more conscious thought to marriage, separation, divorce and parental relationships than most other children. Their predictions for their own futures and their advice to parents or children facing marital breakdown are enlightening. We've heard from Chris, John, Jan and Gail. It's worth adding a little more testimony.

Rita, a university student whose parents split eight years ago, is slim, fair, attractive, logical, reflective. She's twenty-two.

"Well, I'm just not sure about marriage; not a bit sure. For starters it's becoming less important in our society, isn't it? Women don't have to rely on their position in a home and family any more as the only way of having a recognized place in the community. They can do it with a career, or whatever.

"But there's a more important thing: people change. And then they just keep changing and changing. When I was going to school—we lived in southern England then—it just wasn't think-able to not marry; and I agreed. I had the same boyfriend from the time I was eleven until I was seventeen. But he was just too serious. He wanted to get married.

"So we split up and then I lived with Larry for about a year; but he got too serious. It was almost suffocating. So then I met Andy, and we went together for a couple of years, but we didn't live together. And then while we were on a trip—we drove to Spain one summer holiday—*he* wanted to get married. So I just went and got on a plane and came home. How do I know what he'll be like, or what I'll want, in five years, or ten years? People change.

"So now there's this man, he's in advertising. He's about thirty-nine and he was married. He has two kids—but they just visit him. And we have a really terrific relationship, 'cause he doesn't want commitments any more than I do; it's just a lovely, open relationship, with lots of giving but no demanding, no restric-tions. Well, there shouldn't be, should there? He doesn't know how he might change and neither do I, not in the long run. I mean, look how my parents changed, from the time when they got married; I think they're both more interesting now, more mature; but they sure couldn't live together—they just grew in different directions.

"And we might do that, too. So we're not making any commit-ments; I'm just going to leave school and go and live with this man—he's really super—in his apartment in London. And I'll probably take some courses there and go on with my career, because he's perfectly open; he wants me to develop myself any way I wish and he doesn't place any restrictions on me.

"But marriage. I don't think so. Maybe it's OK for some people; or maybe later—much later, when you're really sure."

Janice at nineteen, is very still and watchful; she seems to be listening for melodies, sounds, outside the hearing range of other people who are with her. She speaks slowly, drawing on ten years' experience of life with one parent:

"It's hard to say whether marriage is a good idea. It's like skiing, isn't it? You aren't likely to break a leg if you stay home.

"One thing: I think it should be harder to get married. A lot harder, because then you're going to think a lot more about it; and if you really have to work a lot harder to get married, then maybe it's not going to seem so easy to get out of it, later, if it isn't perfect. That's got to be better for everybody, in the long run. Because there's no two ways about it, it harms, it really harms, always, the children. And it emotionally affects the parents too. So it should be lots harder to get started.

"It's probably getting a bit better. I mean, my father was really old-fashioned; I think he still believes that women should be barefoot and, well, in the kitchen, and pregnant all the time. My mother wanted a career and she went and got it; and I think he really felt threatened by all of that. In that generation, you know, that just didn't go with it, with marriage.

"But nowadays, more than ever, I think most men have been brought up with the idea that a woman is gonna give it all she's got. She's not going to settle for anything less than what she truly wants.

"So, if you want to stay home and simply be a housewife—make that a career in itself—just take care of the house, or your husband and your kids, OK. But if you want a career, I think that's another thing you should work out with any man you might want to live with, or marry. You might change, of course. People change. But I think it's really important to get it straight from the very beginning; with the man. And then you've got to remember that you, the woman—any woman—might change; you might want something different from all that in five or ten years from now. So you have to be really careful."

Alex is twelve years old: "I'll want to get married, someday, I think. But I know, now. It's going to teach me, since my Dad left last year, what can happen. And I'll try not to let it happen.

"If there's any difference between my wife and myself we can just talk about it. Fix it up and not make it worse, because I've learned what can happen.

"And instead of getting into fights every day and going out and getting drunk it will teach me to be good to my family and be good to myself. People who like to fight shouldn't get married. They shouldn't be allowed to get married if they just want to fight. The same with people who get drunk. Getting drunk is no good if you are married. You just shouldn't get married, that's all. You should just stay by yourself and not get married and not bother a lot of other people. That's what I think."

Harold is twenty-four, and has lived alone for seven years after four previous years alone with his mother:

"What I learned is that institutions, all institutions—government, marriage, schools, businesses, whatever—all of them are just a crock, you know? A crock of shit.

"So who wants to live in a crock? Right? You're stuck with some of them—the government, the police, the rules and everything. But why climb into another crock inside the ones you're already stuck with? I ask you.

"I can live like I want to, if I live alone. Eat whenever I want—three a.m., midnight, whenever I feel like it; get my hair cut, someday, if I feel like it. Or not. Wear what I want. Work if I like it. Or not. Right?

"But marriage? No. Then you're stuck, baby. Ever see a married couple who really have fun, really do what they want? Not me. That's why they always split. So me, I got smart, I split, OK, when I was seventeen. No institutions for me. Who wants to live in an institution? Right?"

Alan is thirteen, and very open, sunny, frank and warm in conversation:

"Before I get married I'm going to make sure it's going to work and I'm not going to rush into anything; I'm going to make sure that the person I'm going to marry is right for me and I'm going to try very hard to keep that marriage together, to make it work well.

"I'm not sure how I can really be sure, before I get married, that the person is just right for me. But you really have to try; you have to do everything you can to really be sure and talk about it a lot with that person. Because otherwise it's too dangerous."

Ian is sixteen; a baseball cap neatly bisects kinky, bushy hair that juts out in two large, round puffs of tight curls over each ear; he is lanky, seemingly all elbows, knees, large feet in canvas sneakers and restless, big-wristed hands; he crouches on the floor while we talk, rocking on his heels, arms clasped around his knees:

"As for me—if I find the right girl and I think I'm gonna marry her, then I'm gonna just marry her, that's all. I don't think this has had any effect on me; I doubt it very much; I'm really not too much like him (Ian's father) anyhow. And he was just unlucky, I think; they both were.

"I want to have kids, you know. That's for sure. But it has to be the right time, see? I can't just rush into it.

"I guess there's always the possibility it wouldn't work, the possibility of getting married and having kids and then splitting up. But I can't worry about that; if you worried about that you'd never get married. Anyway, I can't worry about it now; anything can happen, you just have to wait and see. Right now I have to think about other stuff—school, and baseball, I play lots of baseball. So I'm not worried about it now, so much."

Sherry is eleven; short for her age, chunky, rather plain but with a merry smile:

"I'll get married when I grow up, I'm pretty sure. Maybe I'll have a few kids. But I'll be really careful. That's most important. Adults aren't careful enough when they get married. Kids would be more careful. But adults, they don't think about the future—just about then, and what they want right then; they should think about how they're going to use the money, and everything. Or if they're going to get a job. Then it would be OK to be married. But maybe not till they are older; a bit older."

Vincent is fourteen; after seven years' separation his views on marriage are very clear, very dogmatic:

"People shouldn't ever get married because they are pregnant. They've just got to be sure they really want to be married—like they aren't being forced to be or anything like that. So they should just live together for a long time first. Nobody should be allowed to marry until they live together for at least five years, to try it out. Then they'd know. That's what I'm going to do."

Even taking into account replies which vary with age, some feelings are close to universal. Most of the children believed that marriage should be made more difficult. Even toddlers of four and five were clear that "People shouldn't get married unless they really love each other."

A very large majority of these kids are certain that no one should marry until "they are older." Of course "older" varies, widely and wildly, according to the age of the respondent. Little girls of six and seven said solemnly that, "Nobody should get married until they are at least twenty or twenty-two." By ten or twelve years the earliest nuptial age seen as respectable and, above all, "safe" was twenty-five. Teenagers generally stated that, "No one ought to get married until they are grown-up and mature, and know what they want." That "age of maturity" was usually seen as thirty.

Proximity in time to the traumas of the separation related directly to the intensity of conviction that marriage was to be treated with great caution, certainty and commitment. Time seemed to provide opportunity to build rationale (or scar tissue?) and ameliorate an almost Calvinist disapproval of broken marriages—although almost always with the reservation that, "Of course, that doesn't apply to my parents."

Girls interviewed had clearly thought more deeply, more often and more subjectively about marriage than boys; this was most markedly true of girls aged twelve or thirteen and older. No teenaged girls in the interview sample wanted to marry before twenty-three and most felt they would not marry before thirty. Fully a third of these girls said freely that they were very unsure about whether they would ever marry and twenty to twenty-five per cent of these said they simply would not marry, ever.

Most of the girls from twelve to twenty had read and considered the arguments of the women's rights movement and their reaction may partly have stemmed from that. Many, especially those over fifteen regarded themselves as beneficiaries of that movement: "Nowadays women don't have to marry to have respect or financial security. It's even pretty OK to have a child now, without a husband. Anyhow, I'm going to give myself time to develop my own interests first. Then I'll see."

Adolescent boys, conversely, had much more casual subjective responses to marriage. Their generic views mirrored those of the girls; marriage should be later; perhaps waiting periods or trial marriages were a good idea; people ought to be "sure." But most, like Ian on p. 143, were surprisingly relaxed about their own futures: "Sure when I'm ready. I mean, I don't want to have to cook and everything, for myself." "You can't have a good life if you're not married. I will, soon as I'm ready."

Many of the boys' feelings seemed consequent on their fathers' conditions and lifestyles after separation and divorce. They (the sons) had endured badly prepared meals and slovenly housework during "visits with Dad," and wanted no part of that. Many, too, seemed to have some sense that their father was lonely and a subsequent tinge of guilt about seeing too little of the male parent. They didn't want that experience for themselves.

There was a sex difference, too, over the question of having children. Boys, with some atavistic (or just chauvinistic?) sense of race survival, name continuity, ego gratification, help with plough or sabre-tooth hunt or need to breed one's retirement plan, were much more openly interested in having children. Most, though, denied any preference as between boys and girls. (Notable exceptions were boys clearly at odds with their mothers, who wanted sons.)

Many girls simply said they did not want families. Many others said revealingly they "might adopt one or two kids. If I had any of my own I'd only want one. But I think I'd rather adopt some kid who hasn't got a home. Or parents."

All of the adults I interviewed felt the divorce in their childhoods had altered or atrophied their prospects for full and happy marital relationships. Many said they had determined in their youth that they would have no children of their own—had even made that a condition of marriage in later years. Even at forty or fifty years of age and beyond, these former "divorced kids" were fearful of commitment, uncertain as to their ability to maintain enduring relationships. Some, divorced themselves, specifically blamed their parents for their own marital failures; they'd "rushed into marriage to find the emotional security I missed at home" or they had "been conditioned to believe there was no permanence in marriage."

Not one adult in my sample, at any age, regarded the separation of their parents as irrelevant to their own well-being. Most described the event as the most traumatic of their lives (and, astonishingly for me, the sample included some men and women who'd endured much of the worst that World War Two had to offer). Moreover for these adults, memories of the separation and subsequent events were as sharp, clear and painful as yesterday's visit to the dentist.

2. DIVORCE

You are aware by now that most divorced kids generally disapprove of separation and divorce; at the least, they simply don't like it. It hurts.

So much so that Dan, who at fourteen has been a divorced kid for eight years, now says:

"What I worry about is that they're letting too many people get married. And a lot of them don't like each other enough. So they should make it a lot harder to separate, see? And then maybe people would think a lot more about getting married to somebody they didn't like enough."

Kirk is five and he knows with complete conviction that it simply is not necessary for parents to separate. He is sturdy, tow-headed, direct in manner, unself-conscious:

"I think that if something is bothering them they should just tell each other. Then they could stop doing that. But they don't tell each other, and if they don't tell each other then they don't know; so they don't stop doing it. And that's why they fight."

Ellie is twelve. As with many British children, she goes to boarding school; as with some, her attitudes to her parents' problems seem a shade clinical:

"Well, many separations probably really don't exactly have to happen, just occur in the heat of the moment or something. What people should do is take a look at the children, before they break up, and then look at themselves; and if they can see what's going to happen, then maybe they should go to see a psychologist or a marriage counsellor. Perhaps then it wouldn't seem necessary to them. And they could stay together.

"Divorces are very messy, you know. I don't think they are very nice for anybody."

Divisions of opinion over divorce were mostly a matter of age, not sex. Among children under ten, barring those who were brutalized in a drunken or violent marriage, almost all felt divorce was "wrong." They all said divorces should be harder to obtain, should take longer, should involve waiting periods or should, literally, be illegal. "Parents should have to stay with their kids," was phrased again and again.

From age nine or ten up to fourteen, however, the feeling was usually that divorce should be more difficult, but possible. Several youngsters in this age bracket recommended separate holidays, trial separations and marriage counselling. A lot of kids felt a period of marital counselling ought to be a statutory requirement prior to any legal separation: "They should take a holiday by themselves and think it over." "They should wait until they've seen some experts."

Once well into puberty, views changed. Approval, or qualified approval of divorce came mostly from teenagers, one of whom said flatly that "Nobody should think of marriage as permanent. We should just make divorce easier so people wouldn't get hurt so much." (Unhappily, divorces which are legally easy seem not especially easy emotionally.)

Most children into their teens have developed a rationale crisply summarized by Janice: "Look. Here's the question you have to ask yourself: Is it better to be from a broken home, or to be *in* a broken home? So pretty often, separation is best for the kids, even when it's tough for them."

Mid-to-late teenagers were almost unanimous. If there's going to be divorce, it ought to be made quick, easy, inexpensive and, above all, non-adversarial. In this age-range, reactions seemed to bear no relation to the time elapsed since the separation of their own parents. (This differs from views of marriage, as we saw.)

Boys entering early manhood were generally more casual about divorce, just as they were more relaxed about marriage: "Well, sure. I could get divorced. I mean if we just couldn't work it out. But if it doesn't work out, it's better not to be bitter about it; just to end it." "Everybody always wants to blame somebody. That makes me puke. If people can't live together they should just split. It's nobody's fault."

The concept of "no fault" divorce was by far most frequently raised, spontaneously, by boys. There seemed an obvious, unspoken sympathy and identification with fathers who remained their dominant role models; and the fathers were, as is usual in adversarial proceedings, the "guilty" parties, through infidelity or the prevailing social wisdom that the mothers, who will keep the kids, need the family home—so that the male parent "moves out" with all the subsequent possibilities for retroactive notions or claims of "desertion" of family and home.

Apart from these teenagers, the minority comments about easier divorce came from adults. Many of them had married, had children themselves; many had themselves been divorced. As time distances them from the experience of their own parents' divorce, adults tend to regard legal separation and divorce as entirely necessary escape-hatches from the ship of matrimony; they have taken the child's anxiety about how people change, tested it against adult experience and found it true. In that sense they've not changed at all from the time of their adolescence. They are, these adults, somewhat set apart from friends who did not experience a marital disaster in childhood; they remain acutely aware of the pain it can cause. But I was reminded too of a comment made to me, in 1968, by British historian A. J. P. Taylor, during a television interview: "I have found nothing in my studies," said Taylor, "to in any way persuade me that human society has ever learned from experience or from past mistakes." Awareness of the potential for pain and application of that awareness to one's own children can be a light year apart.

3. PARENTS

In the view and experience of divorced kids, most separated parents are "working to rule"—doing no more for their children than the socially acceptable minimum. The kids put it best: "They're just too busy to talk to me, I guess."

It may be that, since *Who's Afraid of Virginia Woolf*, we have stopped kidding ourselves that a civilized veneer necessarily indicates a civilized marriage—or that education, social status and economic comfort are synonymous with warmth, kindness, consideration or politeness. None of us who work and walk in urban settings, watching our fellows change into compulsive egoists once behind the wheels of their autos, would assume the cocktail party personality is the only one in most folks' repertoire. And while researching this book, I've met kids whose gracious, well-tailored Moms are secret drinkers, apprentice sadists or career martyrs, or whose prosperous, charming, successful fathers' treatment of them has been beneath contempt. But we still tend to believe people who regard themselves as sensible, loving, supporting parents. We shouldn't.

A prime reason for the scepticism: divorced kids need all the support they can get—adult support—but too often we "stay away", try to avoid "embarrassing the poor kids," and never, never, ask how they feel, what is happening in their lives.

If approached for advice by divorced parents now, I guess I'd urge them to do what I did: interview some children of other divorced parents. The experience is salutary. The first lesson: you're probably not as good a parent as you suppose—not working as hard at it as you think; those astonishingly rapid gaps in time, when you're preoccupied with work and other things, stretch interminably for your children. The last "real visit" seems like yesterday to you; to them it was precisely seventeen days—and to them that amounts to 408 hours—and 24,480 minutes.

But probably the chief lesson is that, with marital breakdown, change brings opportunity; in this case, opportunity to reassess and strengthen our relationships with our children, and to help them grow up more happily, with less shame and pretence.

It's paradoxical that, in an age when the "how-to" and self-help

149

merchants have a virtual licence to print money, we shy away from most forms of fruitful introspection, looking instead for magical beans in primal therapy, out-of-body experience or fad diets— buying any bizarre philosophy that promises joy without engagement. We're all victims of the Playboy philosophy, personally or at some remove: the notion that "love" can be divorced from interpersonal responsibility. It's a mind-set that British Prime Minister Stanley Baldwin once attributed to the journalists of his day: "Power without responsibility," he said. "The prerogative, throughout history, of the harlot."

But divorced parents *can* learn from reflection, grow from experience. We *can* have loving relationships with our children that will bring rewards infinitely beyond my powers of description, if we just take the time to work a bit at those most seminal of all our activities. None of that works if we proceed with our eyes closed.

One irony I feel in writing this book is that those who might learn and benefit most from the experiences of these kids probably won't read it; they are, of course, those parents who have a separation or divorce looming in their early future, and know it. As one divorced mother told me: "When you've already got more problems than you feel you can handle, the last thing in the world you want is for someone to tell you about a whole new set of problems you should be considering."

So mostly, I suppose, this book will be read, insofar as parents are concerned, by people who, like me, are charter members of the stable-door brigade—people finding out, retrospectively, where their kids feel they screwed up, people trying to mend the holes in their perceptions. But that, too, is respectable. Nor is it ever too late. I don't imagine I can compensate my children for my failure to discuss these things with them from the beginning. But I can at least hope my awareness now provides some sort of retroactive help and feel that we have an infinitely fuller and freer relationship now. I don't play "mea culpa" games with my children, nor do they wish me so to do; but we're a lot better friends for being able, even at this late date, to discuss most of our mutual concerns and experiences with some candour. Several of them have read lengthy portions of this book, approved its tone and substance, and told me they feel that I now understand them a little better.

I do know, now, that my children, and all the other children I interviewed, prefer honest difference of opinion to faked affection. No child wants their parents held hostage to pretence in a deteriorating marriage. It's not difficult to explain to children that pretence is corrosive, that life holds more promise for everyone when tensions are relieved. More positively, children can understand, if we take the time to tell them, that we will have more emotional energy and happiness to share with them, once unburdened of marital discord; but telling alone doesn't make it so. Children are the ultimate pragmatists. We must show them.

MOTHERS

In many respects mothers clearly have the tougher parental role to play after divorce and their extra problems and anxieties are reflected in the perceptions of their children. Some examples of the additional load on divorced mothers:

Most obviously, mothers usually have the day-to-day care of the children and, as the daily disciplinarians, are more often resented.

Despite the many true horror stories of divorced fathers subsisting on virtually no funds while their income goes in alimony and support payments, the vast majority of women living alone with their children have less income than their former spouse, and much more financial worry. (The latest U.S. statistics, for instance, show that median income for female-headed single-parent families is $6,400 annually; for men the figure is $13,800 a year.)

Where separation was initiated by the husband, a lot of divorced women feel wronged: the victims of philandering when that was a mainly male activity; the helpless cast-offs of a society that celebrates young bodies, tip-tilted breasts and bellies free of post-natal stretch marks or post-caesarian sag; the innocent casualties of their husband's menopausal itch; the stumbling blocks in hubby's monstrous career ambitions; the silent martyrs who sacrificed personal development to household duties only to find themselves seen as less interesting than a perky new secretary or a better-educated, more widely-travelled young woman executive. The bitterness shows and colours relations with the kids.

Many divorced mothers fear they will never remarry. The

median age of divorcees is dropping significantly (from 38.5 to 35.6 years of age in a recent four-year span in Canada, for example) but women past thirty still fear their chances in the marriage market. Statistics confirm their fears: in the U.S. four female divorcees in every six remarry—but among men the rate is five out of six.

With that background, here are some general reactions of divorced kids to their mothers.

First, these kids are not, generally, much hurt by or concerned about financial difficulties; they hear too much about such problems and they resent it. Generally they are content to live with reduced expectations; many, in their teens, are happy to work part-time and assist in household expenses. But they do not like what several of them described as "whining" about money. Consultation and positive plans are what they crave.

Second, most divorced kids do not like the chronic criticism of their fathers which their mothers frequently inflict on them; these kids view that catechism of complaint as an affliction, and one not to be happily borne. The war is over. Give them the first benefit of peace: amicable relations.

Third, mothers who attempt to use their children either as spies or message-bearers are much disliked for those causes. "Mom shouldn't try to use us to spy on Dad or beg him. That's not fair; it's forcing us to take sides and we shouldn't have to."

Also children are often aware that their mothers make visits to their father difficult or unpredictable. They need predictability and do not easily forgive this form of interference. (Most dramatically witnessed by children in several overheard telephone conversations between a mother and a father—or a mother's attorney—in which prompt support payments were described as the *quid pro quo* for visits. Divorced parents should have frequent reminders of the amount of data—accurate or, worse, distorted—which children may extract from overhearing one half of an emotional telephone conversation. The threats and predictions may be mainly cathartic for the parent, and soon forgotten. The kids remember.)

On the bright side, the most widely-used phrase among divorced kids asked to describe their mothers was: "She's prettier now." Permutations included: "She dresses nicer." "She laughs a lot more." In the early months children are much more likely to notice how morose their mother has become; but after that adjustment period most are very aware of a "blossoming," and agree it's a good thing.

Some young people detect a deterioration in the pains given to menu planning and meal preparation—but most find meals a happier experience after divorce. Absence of tension is noted along with a feeling of greater closeness with their mother. Moreover for each of those who are the unhappy victims of a mother no longer making special dishes to please a now-absent spouse, there are many more who say, "Mom experiments more now; she tries cooking fun stuff more and that's better for us." All of that, clearly, an adjunct to the blooming phase.

There is, too, a frequent resurgence of "nesting" among separated mothers. It's met with mixed reactions by the children. At least three-quarters of the homes I visited (where the truncated family had stayed on in the marital home) had been redecorated: rooms had been painted in new colours, furniture rearranged, children moved between bedrooms. Generally the children's response to this "new broom" syndrome was one of tolerance; but among a lot of them—particularly those under ten years—there was a sense of disorientation, confusion, even hurt. Stability equals security for divorced kids and a new city, school, home—even a new bedroom or wallpaper, can make adjustment more difficult.

A final observation that runs diametrically contrary to conventional wisdom: I met no children who resented a mother who had begun or resumed a career. The same was generally true for mothers who had begun to go out more in the evenings, the only exceptions coming where the mother was evidently overachieving rather frantically in her liberation from the sexual restrictions of marriage.

With mothers who had taken jobs, children usually said: "She's more interesting now that she's working, takes better care of herself, has a more interesting life and is better to be with when she's at home."

FATHERS
Most complaints about fathers, and they were legion, spring from

absence and from what might stem either from guilt feelings or from an inability or unwillingness to communicate affection.

Fathers have an extremely bad track record for reliability. The tales of children sitting on doorsteps for one, two, three hours are endemic to this slice of our society. More depressing, the kids very rarely reproach their fathers. And remorse is no panacea. The father who turns up late and mumbles "Sorry I'm a little late, kids, but I brought you. . . " is regarded with a mixture of tolerance and contempt. It's this response in fathers, "buying" affection, that children dislike heartily. And it's this response that seems to bespeak either an onerous burden of guilt or a real absence of any skill in communicating warmth except through gifts.

But most vitally, from the kids'-eye view of things, out of sight is truly out of mind. Divorced kids usually assume their fathers may forget birthdays or cancel plans at the last minute. Fathers don't telephone unexpectedly just to chat or say goodnight; if they travel they rarely remember to send postcards, to bring back the souvenirs that used to mark homecomings. Five minutes for a 'phone call or a postcard will pay enormous dividends in their happiness. (There's probably a very lucrative business opportunity available for the entrepreneur who offers a service reminding divorced fathers to call or write to their kids more often or, worse, offers to mail those cards and letters for them.)

The third most commonly expressed complaint of divorced kids is that they never "have a chance to really visit with Dad."

There are two reasons. Most fathers, especially in the early years after divorce, seem to feel impelled to "entertain" their children during parental visits. Publishers of tourist guides to any major city would do well to consult a group of divorced kids: no other comparable segment of our society has so close and frequent an acquaintance with museums, fairs, amusement parks, zoos, and restaurants. Of course kids do like to be taken places. But the happiest visits seem to be on occasions when "We didn't really do anything. We just went to Dad's place and talked and stuff."

A second reason why visits and conversations with the male parent often fall far short of expectations is that frequently "Dad's new girl-friend" is present. And Dad, busy courting, may simply not have much time for his children, nor much patience with them.

Moreover he is not likely to want discussion of matters that remind the new lady of the old; so topics are limited, maybe changed confusingly in mid-sentence.

There are advantages, though, to Dad's new romantic interest, and children quickly note and exploit them. For example, Dad is very unlikely to wish his new "friend" to see in him the stern disciplinarian: kids can get away with more when she's around; they know it, and they do. Also Dad will probably want to be seen, through his lady's eyes, as generous and accommodating; again, kids know the best times to ask for a new bicycle, a trip to the movies, a pizza or two weeks at a special camp.

There can be genuine advantages too. First of all, time spent with the father really can be more concentrated. More time can be "set aside," more activities shared. Most fathers have the great advantage that any day spent with their children can be "special." One caution though. In many, many cases freedom from routine care of the youngsters leads to an unhealthy indulgence: children given bicycles before they are old enough to ride them safely; boys taken on hunting trips before they ought to handle fire-arms; youngsters in their early teens encouraged to "have a drink with me before dinner;" in some cases kids twelve, thirteen and four-teen taken to bars and night clubs, given hugely inappropriate sums of spending money, offered marijuana by a father trying to be "a buddy" to his children—all of this, it must be stressed, by parents, usually fathers, who are intelligent, well-educated and who think of themselves as thoughtful, well-motivated parents.

And how has Dad changed? "He seems a lot younger now." "He goes out more; enjoys himself." As with mothers, fathers are frequently seen as less harrassed after divorce. The wisest of fathers avoid exhibiting the more ostentatious of their efforts to regain lost youth in the early weeks/months after break-up before their children, but do find a less confining lifestyle allows them to share a more casual, less authoritarian relationship with the kids.

Children often are more easy, too, with fathers now less obviously cast as disciplinarians. But what the kids still crave is a visible continuance of interest and concern. Dad may not be around to check on bedtime every night now; but his pride in youthful accomplishment is as vital. When the report card is brought along on the weekend visit the first priority should be to read and comment on it; and when there's an "open house" or parental visiting day at the school, it's worth a few hours away from work to attend. Children are not embarrassed by the presence of the separated parent at such times—they are proud and possessive.

The biggest bonuses for parents of divorced kids come from the smallest acts: the extra 'phone call, the brief letter, the time it takes to attend a swimming meet, school concert or play. Memories of those times are the most precious possessions of divorced kids; they displayed them for me, in our conversations, with all the pride of a freckle-faced boy with his first robin's egg or an aging politician with a favourable public opinion poll.

A final message for the non-custodial parent—the weekend father or mother: build some secure, predictable, private space for your children.

Not every divorced parent, faced with the need to build a whole new (second) home, can afford a separate, private room for a child or children who are present only 50 or 100 days out of each year. But most of us can manage a toybox in a specified corner of the living-room or TV room; can stack a few boards on bricks as a games corner for the kids and stock those shelves with a few books, games, hobby supplies.

Something else about these private spaces: *Share the planning.* That may range from taking the kids along to "shop" to using a scratchpad to plan shelves or a hand-made chest; but *let them participate.*

As with all of us, the need to pee on the trees, to let our peers and enemies know this is "our place" is paramount. A few photos on the walls, some artwork done (at school) by the kids; a chess game or a desk with last week's unfinished model aeroplane or dress pattern: all bespeak continuity, confidence in next week, a belief that things are "normal." My youngest children love these *continuing* projects; the clay models they craft this week are waiting, on *their* bookshelves to be painted next week, when dried; a week later they will be waiting to be varnished; a week later, to be wrapped, combined with a hand-drawn card, delivered to teacher, friend, even the *other* parent, as gifts.

In this area divorce can expand opportunities rather than limiting them. Your kids should have two homes now—not none. So, if your new home is *theirs*, they should feel their friends are welcome. Suggest they bring one along, sometimes, for the weekend; that will make you less remote, mysterious, unreal. Make them, too, feel it really is their home.

4. LOVERS

Most children make little difference between parents who "date" and those who "bed" their new friends. When lovers occur in the singular, divorced kids have relatively few problems with them. There's a major sex difference, though: Dad's new girl-friend is generally liked (she's courting, too, and working at being agreeable). Mom's lover is often seen as domineering.

Outrage is rare, but there are exceptions, the most common apparently when a mother has a succession of lovers, not always in chronological order. Children react much less well to temporary relationships. Teenagers today have an apparently unerring eye for one-night stands; they are contemptuous of them and rarely mistake them, as do their parents, on occasion, for love.

In the most frequent order of things, divorced fathers tend more often to "have someone" on stand-by at the time of separation; mothers, experimenting with their freedom and dating more widely while seeking a satisfying relationship, are much more likely to bring home a succession of "friends" to their children's dismay and discomfiture. Sometimes, having met the mother to arrange permission for interviews, the revelations came as something of a surprise: "She has lots of boy-friends. They are all really young—a lot younger than her or Daddy." "She's a lot nicer to her friends than she was to Daddy." "When she makes lovies we have to stay in our room."

In divorced kids of approximately thirteen and up, the usual feeling about a happy, new romantic relationship for either parent is one of welcome. They often feel their parents have been denied affection, warmth, the thousand small attentions their TV sets tell them are the signals of love and the triggers of happiness. Caught between the romantic idealizations of movies and television and the gritty reality of monochromatic marriage in the pre-separation period, these youngsters are delighted if their mother receives flowers from a new beau or their father shows excitement and anticipation before a "date." At the period in their lives when they most crave romance, their pace has been slowed to the lock-step of restrictive reality; even vicarious romantic adventure brings a quickening thrill—the more so if it carries the justification of a loved parent's progress from bleakness to some visible form of fulfilment.

If your lover is a divorced parent and you wish to avoid problems with the kids—even to make their lives happier—these guidelines:

Don't compete with those kids for the attention or affection of a parent; there ought to be enough to go around and they are acutely sensitive to even subtle variations on this kind of contest.

Don't kid the troops. The children will be aware of the physical aspects of your relationship, in broad terms, just about as soon as you. Slipping away to go home at 4 a.m. won't fool anybody; neither will hiding your dressing gown behind Dad's shirts in the closet.

Never try to buy the kids' love. A small gift is OK as and if it's appropriate. Anything more will only buy you a patronizing package of tolerance.

Don't, ever, ask the children to "Call me Mom." Nothing irritates more quickly nor offends more deeply. And avoid euphemisms; "Uncle George" is silly, and they know it. "George" will do fine.

These young people are interested in your credentials as one who brings pleasure to their parents: they aren't specially scrutinizing *your* parental skills. So tread softly as an arbiter or disciplinarian. If you doubt their wisdom in this matter, reflect on the statistics showing that most police deaths on duty occur while lawmen are attempting to intervene in domestic disputes; there are currents and histories between parent and child of which you can know nothing. Butt out.

Never over-achieve; wait for the kids to come to you.

If you are a divorced parent, you have my enthusiastic permission to cut this page from this book and have it framed for presentation to your lover. It will be an inexpensive and rewarding investment. At least, that's what your kids say.

5. STEP-PARENTS

If you are a recently re-married divorced parent or a "new" step-parent, it may surprise, hurt, offend you a little to find that many divorced kids make little difference between parental lovers and legally sanctioned and contracted step-parents. "Sure. I really hope it works for them. But you never can be sure any more, can you?" Our divorced kids, as we've noted before, are the once-burned cats of our society. So, new step-parent, try not to be angry if you detect an air of watchfulness, of suspended judgment especially from teenaged children of your bride/groom. It's not necessarily that these kids distrust your intentions or expect failure from their "natural" parent. But they don't have a lot of confidence in the "system" any more. You can maybe help them rebuild that confidence; but only with the evidences of time.

There can be no doubt that they matter to the stability of our national communities, these relationships between divorced child and step-parent; there are, in the U.S. alone, about 25 million step-parents; add in the United Kingdom and Canada and the total approaches 35 million.

Feelings towards and about step-parents depend very much on who remarried. In a majority of situations, children respond more positively, less cautiously, when the parent they do not live with remarries. Step-parents so acquired are going to be absentee step-parents and therefore a relatively light burden even if unloved by the children. Often, though, the acceptance is positive, especially from those entering their teens or older: "Dad's made kind of a real home again." "I think she must be good for him; he's a lot more relaxed and happy now."

Some of the problems which, once recognized, can usually be easily dealt with:

The time, energy, money spent in "nesting" with the new spouse are sometimes seen (usually accurately) as subtracting from the resources left for children. Resentments can easily develop around activities ranging from painting the new house or apartment to holidays from which the kids are now excluded. Remedy? Include them.

In a majority of second marriages the step-mother is a good deal younger than the "original." Sometimes this facilitates a relaxed, peer-like relationship with older children; but it can create tensions when kids have trouble demonstrating as much "respect" as their father may expect for his young bride.

If there are children in a second marriage, only emotionally secure youngsters from the first union will escape some sense of demotion, of parental affections spread thin. These anxieties can be brutally exacerbated if their other parent expresses resentment of the "new" family. Don't do it.

Finally, the custodial parent sometimes reacts with great bitterness to a marriage. Such responses were fairly rare in my sample—more often there was a relaxation of former hostility to "girl friends"—but where anger over the new bride was exhibited, it caused corrosive conflicts of loyalty for the children. Their dilemma was often multiplied by a complete ignorance in the step-parent of the pressures on these kids.

Remarriage by the custodial parent (usually the mother) poses more problems, for obvious reasons:

The children rely much more on this parent for emotional support; they fear any attrition of that and need reassurance.

The custodial parent is there daily, the only parent available to help, with homework, hair styling, personal projects of any kind. A step-parent should double the available help, of course; often they do. But the fear of distracted attention in the "natural" parent is greater with a step-parent "at home."

Step-parents living with divorced kids have far more temptation to take part in discipline and far more risk, thereby, of incurring resentment. Don't heat up this area of friction by being over-protective of the custodial parent and suggesting he/she is being "taken advantage of" by the kids.

Problems always have a higher profile than pleasures; in fact more than half the step-parental relationships I encountered seemed, on balance, to stimulate more contentment than resentment. There were often obvious and positive benefits:

Step-parents living with the custodial parent often supplied the missing male companionship so needed.

Often step-parents do provide incremental time and attention for children. This extra emotional support and affection, when it wasn't intrusive or ham-fisted, was a clear and vital plus.

At the most pragmatic level, step-parents often share household chores, so that there's less cooking and cleaning; fewer repair jobs that were anyway beyond the children's experience, strength, skill.

A little rather obvious advice for step-parents:

Affection will develop least painfully if it is offered gently, without demands, conditions, schedules. Be sure the children know if you care for them; but understand that their *pro forma* affection of today will generate bile and anger next year. Be patient; when they are ready for a hug, a good night kiss, you'll know. Be aware that the older they are, the longer the process will take; older children have more self-awareness, more dignity to lose, more fear of initiatives, new ventures.

If the children live with the "other" parent, not your new spouse, try to be sure they have a secure sense of "place" when they visit.

Try to let the children have some private time with their "natural" parent.

Don't be afraid to let your affection for their parent show.

Never, however great the provocation, compete with that other mother/father, the one without the hyphenated relations. Remember that "Those whom the gods would destroy, they first make mad." And that's madness. Always.

Learn to bite down a little, particularly with very young children, the ones who say such things as: "That's not how Mommy does it," and "Now can I 'phone Daddy and ask him if I can stay up later?" Cruelty in small children is unthinking and unknowing; the chances that they were programmed to hurt you by "her" or "him" are very, very remote. In any event, biting back won't help your relations with them—or with your new bride/groom.

Go back one space and re-read the previous section on lovers.
You are one, aren't you, despite marriage?

6. SIBLINGS

The vast majority of divorced kids come from families of two
children or more. It's difficult from my closeness to the children
and the subject, to decide whether their most common interpersonal feelings are cause for jubilation or for sadness: jubilation,
because these children, much more than "married" kids, are enormously sensitive to one another and mutually supportive far
beyond our usual social norms; sadness, because that mutual support seems often to take the form of "us against the world" and even
of "us against them," with "them" being both parents.

In the most common situation, where all the children are with
one parent, the most usual sign of the divorce is this heightened
concern. It is in this area, more than any other, that I believe
divorced kids mature, in the best sense, more quickly than most.
With one parent gone and the other often working or self-
preoccupied, there are many times when there is simply no parent
available to dry tears, soothe scrapes, contend with the tiny hurts
that can lacerate a child's day. Most divorced kids seem quicker to
notice a hurt in a brother or sister, and more willing to take the time
to lend support.

Of course a good deal of the expressed concern of one child for
another invites the educated guess that there's a lot of transference
going on: "I'm really worried about my older sister. She really can't
handle it, you know." "I'm OK. But my little brother is really
mixed up. He doesn't understand and he feels frightened." "Well,
I'm the oldest so I try to kind of take the place of a father. I mean try
to settle arguments between them, explain to them that it's really
going to be OK for us."

Sometimes, too, the extra concern can lead to resentments, as in
Dawn, now sixteen and living with her mother and an older
brother:
    "Well, he's two years older than me; and so he was twelve
when they split up, and he'd try to take over the father's role; I

mean, he'd make our lunch, usually, and then he'd try to discipline me a lot. He got too big for his shoes, I thought."

Or in May who's nine:
"One thing: if Mom and Dad still lived together my sister and I wouldn't have Jack bossing us around all the time. My sister and I talk about that a lot; it's like he's trying to be the father."

(Jack sees things a little differently; he is protective towards his sisters, but not enthused about his surrogate paternal role: "Well, I have to spend a lot of time helping my sisters, and looking after them. If they have a problem at school, if maybe someone is chasing them around, I have to help them, 'cause Dad isn't around to do it. And I have to come home early from school to baby-sit them, and I really hate doing that. If my father were here my mother wouldn't have to go to work, and then I wouldn't have to baby-sit and make meals and stuff and I could go and stay with my friends after school.")

Much more often, though, there is a real shared compassion. I've seen a degree of mutual support and concern among my own children which I find astonishing and enormously healthy.

In terms of positive advice, it's clearly in the interest of every child for parents to encourage shared activity, sympathy, loyalty between the children of any ruptured family. The need for that sort of encouragement is particularly clear when not all the children still live at home (as when some are away at school or have left for jobs or marriage) or when not all of the children live with the same parent.

Where children are separated in custody splits, even when they have been allowed to choose the parent with whom they'll live, there is often a double sense of loss and a yearning to see more of the absent brother(s) or sister(s).

Richard, seventeen, whose younger sisters live with his mother while he is with his father, said: "What's really strange, especially at night, after supper, is, you look around, and you don't see any little kids running around, having fun. I really miss them."

And they miss him. Said one: "I see Richard at the community centre sometimes 'cause we both go to the same one; and once I saw him at the library, too. But it really isn't the same. He used to tease me a lot, and bug me, but I didn't really mind him all that much. I sure miss him."

Often, too, there's a sense of guilt amongst children in their teens who feel they don't try hard enough to spend time visiting siblings living with the other parent.

"I feel as though I ought to go and see them more; they are younger and need lots of love; but I feel so uncomfortable there— like a spy from the enemy camp. It's as if Mom can't forgive me for staying with Dad, even though she said we should all choose."

Advice comes from Sue, who's fourteen, and lives with her father and an elder brother; two younger sisters live with her mother:

"The main thing for parents is to let their kids visit each other a lot, make it easy for them. I think a lot of the time the parents think the kids they have belong to them; and maybe they almost resent the kids the other parent has. It's as if they thought we might catch something from each other, as if living with your other parent is like having measles at the time, for this parent. So kids have to really be sure they stay close."

Relations between siblings, however, are infinitely variable, as they are in "complete" families. There are exceptions to the mutual support pacts in those self-sentenced social exiles who, like serious burn victims, can't risk the pain of touching or being touched; and there are exceptions too when brothers and sisters are divided either by custody or by having "taken sides." Where custody of two or more youngsters is split it is generally the older children who live with the father—more often boys than girls. In these situations the normal patterns of squabbling, failed understanding and impatience exhibited in "complete" families between children several years (or one sex) apart can be exaggerated.

Sometimes resentments build. Jenny, now almost twenty, and three other children stayed with their mother while their two-years-older sister went with her father:

"I think she was always his pet; the oldest, you know; and she always took his side in all the fights around here. And she just went with him. The rest of us—we tried not to take sides at all and, of course, we weren't asked where we wanted to go."

Where only one of several children living with one parent is particularly sympathetic to the absent parent, often there is bitterness:

"My older sister is always sucking up to my father. I guess she was always his favourite anyhow. She never seems to understand the problems my mother has. I like him, for sure, but I get sick of the way she's always going around there."

"My younger brother went to stay with Dad for a while, a whole summer. And Dad asked him if he'd like a motorcycle and said he'd buy him one if he stayed; and they used to go drinking in the pub together every night and yack and stuff. He just took Dad for everything he could. Dad knew what he was doing, too. He said once my brother was as cunning as a shithouse rat. But he didn't care, he wanted company. Me, though, when I was there, I just couldn't take that stuff, remembering how Dad never helped Mom support us when we were young. I think my brother is more like my Dad. I guess that's all right. For him."

Basically, however, sibling relationships survive pretty well, though with all their need to share and discuss their feelings, it seems divorced kids almost never talk about their experiences even with their own brothers and sisters. A couple of suggestions here:

On a few occasions when two or more of my children have discussed the consequences of divorce with me, together, there's been an obvious and useful sharing of information and pooling of response. Such conversations, casually encouraged, seem very beneficial.

It seems clear too that children who tend naturally to have more sympathy or common interests with one parent, should be encouraged by that parent to increase their time with the other parent. If lop-sided loyalties and tensions of the kind we've witnessed between children are allowed to build, everyone loses.

7. EXTENDED FAMILY

Finally, let's step outside domestic confines.

For most divorced kids, the world is divided, like Caesar's

Gaul, into three parts: first, their parents; second, all the individuals who touch them closely or regularly; finally, everybody else.

Generally "everybody else" is regarded as of no interest insofar as perceptions of altered lifestyle are concerned. And in the second category, even with close friends, most divorced kids regard their family situation as a closed book. (Schoolteachers are even less entitled to any knowledge or involvement. When asked whether teachers are aware of their changed status, most divorced children answer simply, "It isn't any of their business.")

Relatives, though, have a crucial role to play. My assumption is that many people—grandparents, aunts and uncles, neighbours and friends of divorced kids and their parents—will read this book hoping to gain some insight into the problems of these youngsters. The most essential insight is simply that parents aren't, after divorce, all that great; other adult company and friendship is needed. And the obvious is true, that extended family members— aunts, uncles, grandparents—are ideally situated to play an enormously supportive role.

In reality, though, many do damn little or nothing about it: "No, I've never asked about it. It would embarrass them." "I wouldn't dream of raising it. I don't think they could handle it." Fear of interference can lead to them having almost no contact. Even worse, kids told me of relatives who "take sides." That embarrasses the kids and renders any relationship uncomfortable, maybe even destructive. I have stories of grandparents living a half-dozen city blocks away who never phoned, wrote, visited the children because, paternal relatives, they blamed the mother for the separation and refused to see her. Then there are the cousins forbidden to play with these children of divorce evidently in the belief the social disease may prove contagious. The Old Testament injunction about the sins of the fathers was never more cruelly demonstrated. It's those relatives who fix blame, insist on maintaining an adversarial posture, who most offend and distress these kids.

There are many, many exceptions: uncles who turn up often and provide much-needed male companionship; grandparents who do write, 'phone, visit, take time to play games and tell stories about "the olden days." Youngsters so blessed show it; they are perceptibly happier. All it takes is the investment of a little time and energy. If adult relatives or family friends would occasionally take a divorced child to a film or on a picnic (without making it seem a charitable activity) much of the problem would evaporate.

I met one little boy who, in his entire eight years, had never enjoyed the thrill of flying a kite. (His parents had separated when he was about three.) He wasn't seriously scarred by that small hole in his experience, but it stood for the gap in his life. He'd probably be a much happier adult, one day, if someone took him kite flying (by preference having first built, not bought, a kit with him) a couple of times this summer.

One of my own sons told me his greatest resentment had been, for years, that there was no man to whom he could look for help with problems like repairing his bicycle or putting together some bookshelves in his bedroom. Because my visits with him, in those years, were "scheduled" and were in my home not in his, I was simply not "on call."

The geography of parental visits is one reason the support of adult extended family members is so crucial. It's a rare divorced couple who are comfortable together—comfortable even having their absent spouse visiting children in the original home. But most of the everyday problems with which children need adult guidance occur "at home," and it's there the extra adult support is wanted.

Adult relatives can supply something beyond simple role models or advice about the care and feeding of a pet guinea pig. They have a running start on any other adults wishing to help because they are known quantities, trusted and loved individuals. It's especially important that relatives of the non-custodial parent maintain and strengthen their relationships with these children thereby demonstrating that the marital breakdown has not branded either parent as a pariah or made the children untouchable. The best-adjusted children with whom I spoke almost invariably told me of an aunt or uncle, a grandparent or adult cousin with whom they often met and talked. They often feel comfortable sharing their feelings with an adult relative who has had no direct part in the conflict but has made clear their continuing and non-judgmental affection.

Since extended family members live outside the constraints of formally-scheduled visits, their "casual" continuing relationships have even more validity for the children. Given the ease with which divorced kids can be included in the ordinary activities of aunts, uncles, grandparents there seems no conceivable excuse why this simple, joyful form of preventive spiritual medicine should be denied any child of divorce. Bystander apathy was never less easy to excuse nor more easy to avoid.

8. FRIENDS; BOY-FRIENDS; GIRL-FRIENDS

FRIENDS

Obviously it helps if a divorced kid has friends. This is the most woolly area in my research tapes, the one where answers were most elliptical, least forthcoming, but I think I can hazard a few broad conclusions:

Among children under, say, eight years of age, there seemed little self-consciousness with friends in respect of their "divorced" status. But between eight and fourteen there was widespread embarrassment. More than half these children told me they had not "confessed" their changed situation to their friends; some who had moved said they were hoping none of their new friends would learn of their situation. A few, particularly girls, said they never invited friends home for fear they would learn of the implied deception. Others lied, told friends who visited that their father was "away on business."

Once well into their teens, most girls seemed to have one close girl-friend with whom they discussed their home life. Often they said they maintained the conspiracy of silence with everyone else. Teen-aged boys expressed less conscious need for a confidant, though many seemed to have one.

Several children spoke of "moving away" when they finished school so as to escape associations where their friends knew of their circumstances. Many adults I interviewed said they had never spoken of the divorce; tried to keep the scar hidden under the bright clothing of "normalcy." Perhaps one day the sheer number of divorced kids in the world will erode the need most of them feel for secrecy with their friends. But that will be a big change.

BOY-FRIENDS AND GIRL-FRIENDS

It's harder to keep secrets from those you're dating. If my sample is representative there is a sex difference here, and a typical approach to dating and going steady that is, compared to the social norm, aberrant. Bear in mind, however, that divorced kids are already approaching 40 per cent of our youthful population; they are a huge minority group and they're busy building their own norms— norms that will affect us all.

Boys tend to date later, to show interest in girls and all that goes with them at a later age. The exceptions seem to be those who feel no affection to speak of at home, or from the absent parent, and who seek early romance for emotional security. These few exceptions are likely to marry early, almost desperately, as a way to "get out" of an intolerable home situation. But most teenage boys seemed more likely to plunge into athletics and other hobbies in a much more than average spirit of dedication.

Girls seem, more than boys, to suffer emotional dislocation and deprivation following divorce. (Is my chauvinism showing? I don't know.) Certainly adolescent girls *talk more* of such problems. They seemed to me to be especially vulnerable to any promise of emotional support. Ironically, they couple this clear need with a firm conviction that they want no commitments. Like a hyper-anxious small child, afraid to play with a seductive toy because it might break, these youngsters fear commitments (and through their fear seem doubly easy for unscrupulous young men to victimize). A common story from girls of between fifteen and twenty years of age was of a romance broken off because a boy-friend was too intrusive, too anxious for commitment, too serious.

Many of these girls are perfectly well adjusted. (Yours, of course?) But most are pathetically eager for a word or gesture of attention or affection. They mask that need only from their parents, whom they fear to "trouble." They all need to love, and want to. But most find trust a more distant goal. Most have been badly scarred by the failure of that institution which, despite Women's Liberation and equal rights movements, is still buried well under their skins as an ideal. Those more articulate say they prefer "civilized relationships" and "open relationships." Even those who've married speak of "not demanding too much," and "keeping lots of private space." If one of them is your lover, girl-friend, wife, be advised she will be far from belief in happy endings; in her fairy tale any prince may turn back into a toad, any time.

An apparent paradox: in my sample the scars seemed deepest in girls of eighteen, nineteen, twenty. I've no explanation of that phenomenon—but a hesitant theory. These young women gave evidence of having believed themselves deeply involved, "in love," immediately prior to their parents' separation. It may be that, at the moment in their lives when they were making their own first serious emotional commitment, they were doubly injured by the shock of failed love. Certainly this group was, to my great surprise, the most hurt, most bitter, least forthcoming segment of my sample.

A final "guesstimate" about the way in which teen-aged divorced kids select boy-friends/girl-friends. I've no scientific evidence but a strong conviction that many of these youngsters, feeling themselves less than whole, deliberately seek other young people who are patently in a worse emotional state than themselves. Students of the Don Juan syndrome claim the most vicious (and successful) philanderers deliberately seek out and seduce women who are emotionally disabled. In something like a similar fashion I believe many children of divorce look for romance among young people who seem to have even less confidence than themselves.

Someone more dependent is "safer," less likely to disappoint; someone who is less attractive is less likely to "stray," maybe as Dad did, or Mom; by attending to someone else's broken wing one may forget the emotional bruises that lie closer to home for a while. I think, from experiences they related to me, that those injured by separation and divorce respond to other initiates in the fellowship of the socially disadvantaged, and that they "cluster," to no one's benefit.

Unhappily, as evidenced by interviews with many adults, such "attractions" frequently lead to marriages which are themselves doomed as the original divorced kids mature, develop a greater measure of self-respect and lose their need for the gratification and security of having a weaker, dependent object for their affection.

As we've seen, many divorced kids are sceptical of marriage while others develop an almost mystical set of convictions about the need to keep it inviolate. There are, clearly, two extreme reactions: one is to regard marriage as a snare, a mortal danger to be avoided at any cost; the other is to seek an early marriage both for security and to show that they do not share the "flaw" in the parents' characters. While there's likely some element of one such response buried in the psyche of every adult child of divorce, these extreme reactions are still the exceptions and probably embrace only fifteen to twenty per cent of divorced kids.

But lack of exaggerated reaction does not mean *no* reaction. So if you marry someone who lived through a divorce in their child-hood or adolescence be advised that they do have some special needs: not greatly different in kind from those we all experience, but almost certainly more profoundly felt—and with priorities-of-need which may vary substantially.

Some examples:

Divorced kids often, as adults, need and want a much more open marital relationship than that which they experienced as children. They may well be ready for more honesty, candour, sharing than many of us who lack their experience of the conse-quences of bottled-up anxieties and frustrations. To the degree this need is realized it can only make your marriage to them more joyful and healthy; so indulge them for your own sake.

They often have a greater-than-average need for emotional security and reassurance. They want reminders of affection, of stability. Every family tends to build its own traditions around festive occasions, holidays, weekends together; those small proofs of continuity mean even more to children of divorce than most folk. So if your marriage is so far childless, for example, it's likely a far better idea to build a sense of "home" by having some friends or relatives stay with you at Christmas than to develop a "where shall we go this year?" approach. Every divorced child begins with some fear of rootlessness; don't add to it.

You probably have a better than ordinary possibility of having a very full, shared relationship with your children if your spouse came from a shattered marriage; divorced kids are acutely aware of the value of including *both* parents in times with the kids. Just as professional athletes, from their concentrated experience of observing their own bodies, can probably teach us things about our physical make-up, so a divorced child who's reflected on his/her own experience often has a more conscious and direct sense of a child's emotional needs.

Sometimes divorced kids find it harder than most of us to express affection. They've been burned and they need, above all, patience. Don't hold them too tightly or demand too much, too soon. Also they are experts at separating good intentions from real commitment. That means their commitment to you may be a good deal more mature and more rewarding than you anticipated, understood or even deserved. Be good to them; you are lucky to have their trust and their love; it's not given lightly.

9. THEMSELVES AND THE COMMUNITY

I gave earlier my belief that divorced kids think more about marriage and divorce. What I know for certain is that *divorced kids think they think a lot more about marriage and divorce*. That's an important distinction. The self-perception of many Jews, blacks, Catholics is that *their agony* is unique; the discriminations inflicted on *them* feel special, different. So with divorced kids. Children who have lost one parent through death may have problems that are akin; worse even, in the sense they can never see the absent parent. But "widowed kids" don't have the self-consciousness of divorced kids; there's generally no sense of guilt or shame. Kids in complete families have problems of communication too; but, again, they lack the sense of being set apart, singled out.

One needn't study much psychology or philosophy to conclude that *perception is reality*. Divorced kids *see themselves as different*. So they are. Most of them feel afflicted by a form of social stigma. They don't like it and so they try, often, to obscure the cause, to pretend they are "normal." It's time we told them that, in England and Wales and California—in Toronto, Paris, New York, Moscow, Vancouver, Denver, Stockholm, Calgary, Auckland and Manchester, they are "normal"—at least in the sense that there are now just about as many of them as of the "other kind."

The other pervasive problem is that about one third of all the kids I interviewed said openly that they felt guilt over the divorce—usually irrational, even to them. Another third protested so vehemently when I asked the question as to leave me persuaded it was an acute problem for them, too. All children have occasionally wished ill fortune on a parent. To see major disaster strike their own family is, for many, to see their worst and most guilt-ridden wish-fulfilment come true.

Some divorced kids, as we have seen, learn from blundering parents that their conception "forced" their parents' marriage. Still others feel there would have been less marital strain, more romance, had it not been for their existence. Most kids added "I know it's probably silly." So are addictions to cigarettes, booze, tranquillizers; but those sillinesses are treated seriously in our society, and assisted where help is accepted. These kids need at least the help of communication, and definite assurance from their parents they had no responsibility in the marriage breakdown.

Many of the children's problems are compounded by the society in which we live. I've been constantly reminded of two young psychiatrists whom I met in the late Sixties, while making a documentary film about a huge medical complex. Compressed and paraphrased, this is what they told me in an earnest conversation over several cups of coffee:

"We spent fifteen years learning our trade; we even went through analysis ourselves. And all of our training was of the traditional psychiatric type: we were trained to help people who were screwed-up learn to adapt to and cope with all the constants in their lives: jobs, homes, families, communities.

"Then we came here to practice, and what did we find? We found people whose problems were triggered by an absence of constants. They weren't having trouble coping with the constant factors in their lives at all: they didn't have any. What we have to deal with out here in the real world is a whole new society; everything is fluid today—jobs, families, homes, communities— the works. And nobody trained us to deal with that problem."

This book has been chiefly concerned with children whose "divorces" occurred in the middle class; young people who expected stability, a modicum of physical security and a maximum of emotional and social support. It's trite, but true, that industrial democracies need their middle classes as social stabilizers; true, too, that no middle class can endure without that "climate of confidence" so beloved by government economists. People without confidence in a secure tomorrow have no reason to plan or save, invest or organize, vote or obey the more irksome strictures of law. And divorced kids have less confidence than others in social institutions. The one most sacred and precious to them has failed, and this can't help but have an impact on their relationships with other community institutions. If the implied parental promise "I will always be here to help you, comfort you, support you . . ." can't be trusted, why should these kids believe journalists, teachers, politicians, clergymen?

We're fast approaching the time when half our society will comprise grown-up divorced kids. We need to think about the consequences for us all, because people who expect too little aren't much good at contributing, either. Realism and scepticism are useful personal and social tools; but they can be blunted by a false notion that disappointment is the necessary end of every human endeavour. And apathy, a disease which many of our children have caught, can kill the body politic. Our children need to see our faith in new beginnings and the endurance of hope. They need, too, an understanding of the continuing dependability of parental love and support.

Divorced kids' faith in other people has been eroded and we have to rebuild it. It's essential, for example, for them to see amiability between their separated parents. Divorced parents need not be petty, bitter, vindictive; they should suppress every temptation to surrender to those responses, because the kids will notice them, every time.

Another most crucial lesson, I now think, is to avoid any and all temptations to "negative conditioning." It's worth deliberate effort to remind divorced kids that there are happy marriages, fulfilling relationships, happy endings. One really silly phenomenon encountered by divorced kids centres on their visits to friends' homes where the marriage is intact. Such families sometimes feel it's kinder to suppress evidence of affection and happiness. Nothing makes less sense. Divorced kids need demonstrations that marriage can work, that adults often have loving and fulfilling relationships.

They need to be persuaded that the failure of a single marriage does not demonstrate the inability of adults to have an enduring and satisfying relationship. Our lazy tendency to generalize from a particular is probably never more dangerous.

We can help our children avoid that trap simply by listening to their needs as they have expressed them here, and heeding their pleas for consideration, help, understanding. Marriages can work; often they do. We should remind divorced kids of that fact, show them success stories every chance we get. And parents do go on loving their children even though marriages end. We should give our children constant proof that's true.